The Book of Dolphins

Written and Photographed by
MARK CARWARDINE

C&B
COLLINS & BROWN

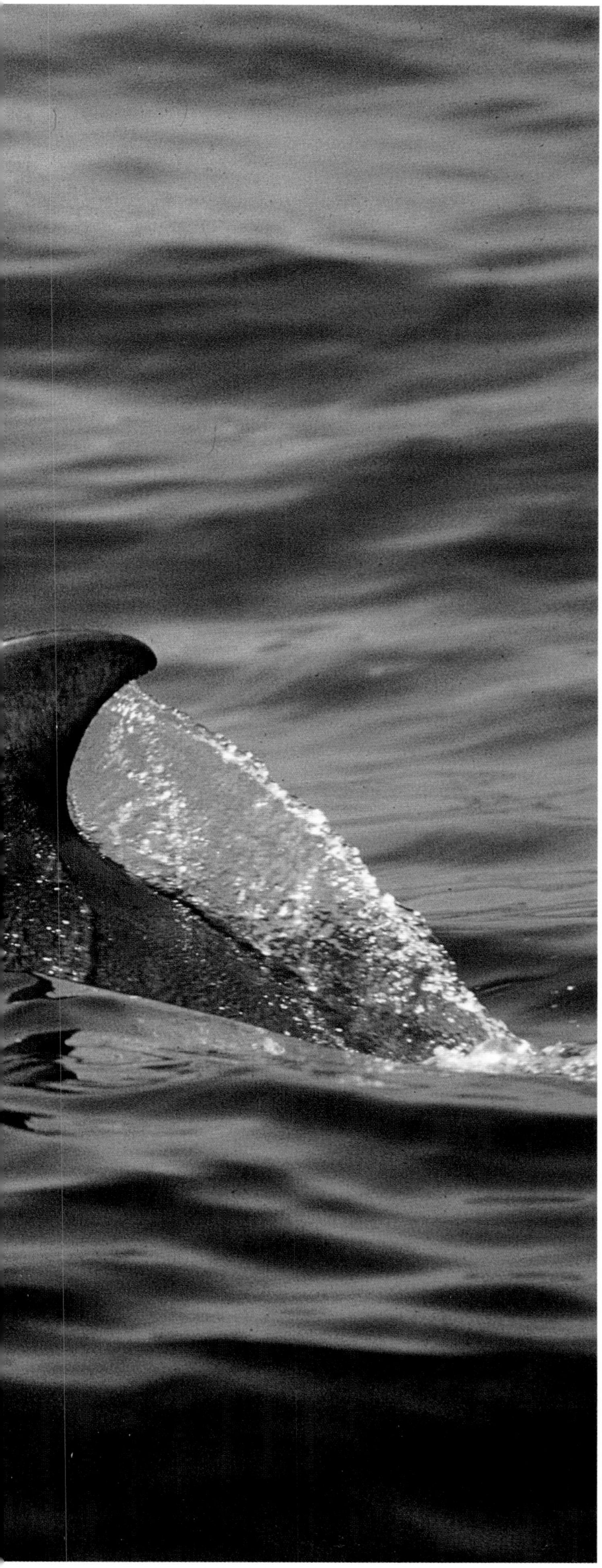

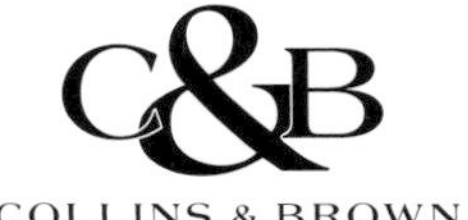

Collins & Brown Limited,
London House,
Great Eastern Wharf,
Parkgate Road,
London SW11 4NQ

First published in hardback in Great Britain in 1996
by Dragon's World Limited

First published in paperback in Great Britain in 1999
by Collins & Brown Limited

Distributed in the United States and Canada by Sterling Publishing Co.,
387 Park Avenue South,
New York,
NY 10016, USA

3 5 7 9 8 6 4 2

British Library Cataloguing-in-Publication Data
A catalogue record for this book is available from the British Library

ISBN 1 85585 737 5 (paperback)

EDITOR: Jane Hurd-Cosgrave

ART DIRECTOR: John Strange

DESIGN: James Lawrence

EDITORIAL DIRECTOR: Pippa Rubinstein

DTP MANAGER: Michael Burgess

Printed in Hong Kong/China

Contents

Foreword
by David Bellamy

Some sixty-five million years ago, a strange group of animals discovered the joys of life beside the seaside. In a remarkably short space of time, they evolved to become dolphins and other members of the whale family – and were soon ruling five-sevenths of the planet.

Sixty million years later, our own ancestors began to emerge. They evolved into Homo sapiens, and came to rule the remaining two-sevenths of the planet.

Yet, in our arrogance, we called this shared home 'Earth'. While the dolphins have always exploited its resources sustainably, we have treated the planet as if it is our own – with scant regard for our fellow inhabitants. Ultimately, of course, if we are incapable of looking after animals as charismatic and intelligent as dolphins, what hope is there of looking after all the others? And what hope is there of looking after ourselves?

Well, there is hope. There will always be hope as long as we take an interest in the natural word around us and appreciate our fellow inhabitants for their true worth.

This is what I like about this superb book. It's not a 'doom and gloom' catalogue of destruction, but a celebration of the magic of dolphins – and a warning of severe problems to come if we don't change our ways.

It gives me great pleasure to write this foreword. The Book of Dolphins brings back many happy memories of watching dolphins with Mark Carwardine, in the wilds of the Arctic and from the sunny shores of Madagascar, and of swimming with several species in other parts of the world. It is always such a privilege to encounter these remarkable creatures in the wild.

Please read this book and enjoy the photographs; if it does not convince you that dolphins are worth saving, then nothing else will.

—David Bellamy
Bedburn, Co. Durham, England 1996

Spotted dolphins, The Bahamas.

Introduction

There is something special about dolphins. It is difficult to put into words, and impossible to prove, yet it is a feeling that a great many people have after a close encounter with one of these enigmatic creatures.

Perhaps it is because we see them as intelligent beings – our equals? Or because they are air-breathing mammals, like us, and yet they thrive in an alien underwater world? Perhaps we are a little jealous and in awe of them because they are able to explore places that are off-limits to us, experience things we will never experience, and see things we may never see? Perhaps it is because we see them as we would like to see ourselves – graceful, compassionate, peaceful, free, full of energy and fun-loving? Or is it simply their fixed 'smiles', which make them appear eternally pleased to see us?

As with so many questions about dolphins, there are no simple answers. Undoubtedly, this sense of the unknown is itself a major part of their appeal. The more we learn about them, the more we realize there is yet more to learn – and the more intriguing their story becomes. While many of our early assumptions about them are no longer considered to be entirely accurate, the 'real' animals are at least as charismatic, captivating and interesting as the quintessential ones we have developed in our minds.

The aim of this book is to summarize our current knowledge of the oceanic dolphins – the twenty-seven 'typical' members in the family Delphinidae. It examines their evolution, biology and natural history. It looks for clues to some of the curious biological puzzles that make them shrouded in mystery: How do they sleep? Why do they strand on beaches? Are they as intelligent as humans? And why do they always seem to be playing? It also explores our relationship with dolphins – how we study them; whether we will ever be able to talk to them; why they seem to enjoy our company, and we theirs; if they can trigger the healing process in people who are mentally or physically unwell; and why they appear to lack human vices such as greed, malice, jealousy and fear.

The relationship between humans and dolphins is an ambiguous one. Dolphins have come to symbolize mystery, serenity and freedom, and have inspired poets, writers, musicians and artists around the world for centuries. We hold them in high esteem. Yet we also imprison them in small concrete tanks, train them to carry out military tasks considered too dangerous for people, routinely kill them for food, drown them in fishing nets, and pollute and destroy their homes. With this in mind, a major portion of this book is also dedicated to the conservation of dolphins.

Above all, the book is a celebration of dolphins: their surprising diversity, mystery, spectacular acrobatics, extraordinary social systems, remarkable adaptations to life in the sea, and much more.

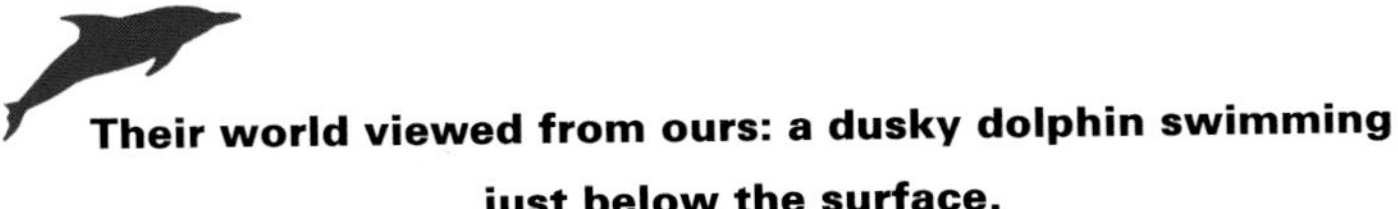

Their world viewed from ours: a dusky dolphin swimming just below the surface.

CHAPTER

1

The Dolphin Family

The oceanic dolphins form the largest group of all the world's whales, dolphins and porpoises. Twenty-seven species are currently recognized by most experts – plus a further six which are more commonly referred to as whales. They live in seas, oceans and many major rivers around the world, from the warm waters of the tropics to the cold waters of the poles.

Dusky dolphin, New Zealand.

One of the strangest things about spotted dolphins is that not all of them have spots: the number and size of spots varies from one individual to another, and according to their age and where they live.

The Diversity of Dolphins

The most familiar member of the dolphin family, and the species most people think of when the word 'dolphin' is mentioned, is undoubtedly the bottlenose dolphin. This is the archetypal dolphin, made famous by the 1960s TV series *Flipper* and by display animals in dozens of marine parks and zoos around the world. But there are a surprising number of variations on this familiar theme and, while dolphins inevitably share many common features, they also come in an impressive variety of shapes, sizes and colours, and have developed many different ways of surviving in the hostile marine environment.

They range from the tiny black dolphin and the equally small Hector's dolphin, each as little as 1.2 metres (4 feet) in length, to the Risso's dolphin, a veritable giant which can grow to an impressive 3.8 metres (12 feet 6 inches). Some species are highly conspicuous, with spectacular spots, brightly coloured stripes, or striking black and white markings, while a few are relatively drab and grey. Some are long and slender and have prominent beaks, while others are much stockier and have poorly defined beaks. Some have large, scythe-shaped dorsal fins, others have small triangular fins, and two have no fins at all.

Dolphin body patterns and shapes also vary between individuals of the same species: the sexes sometimes look different; youngsters frequently change in appearance as they grow older; and there can be many variations between populations living in different parts of the world. Even individuals of the same

species, sex and age, and who live together in the same population, are rarely identical. This can make it surprisingly difficult to tell one species from another at sea – especially at a distance or in poor weather conditions – but it is one of the many challenges that make dolphin watching so enjoyable.

There are a great many other variations and differences between the species. Some live close to shore, and even enter rivers or estuaries, while others occur far out to sea and may never set eyes on land during their entire lives. Some of them are fairly common and widely distributed around the world, but there are others which survive only in small numbers and have much more restricted ranges. Some are highly active at the surface, frequently breaching and splashing, while others are more inconspicuous and prefer to keep themselves to themselves. There are even differences in their choice of food: the majority feed almost exclusively on fish or squid, but a number have much more cosmopolitan diets.

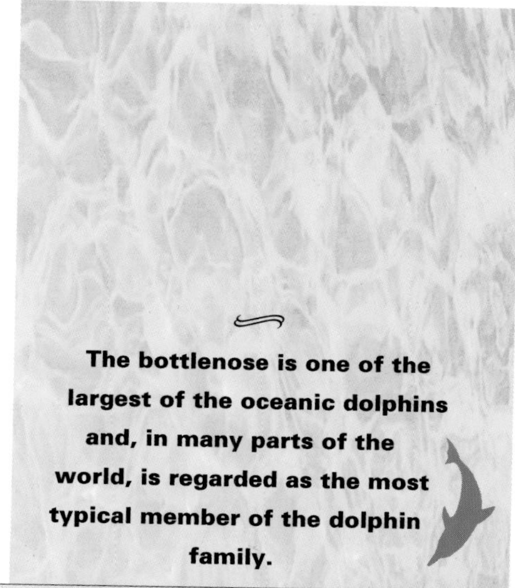

The bottlenose is one of the largest of the oceanic dolphins and, in many parts of the world, is regarded as the most typical member of the dolphin family.

Is it a Whale? A Dolphin? Or a Porpoise?

Animal names can be confusing at the best of times, but whales, dolphins and porpoises are in a league of their own.

Broadly speaking, the word 'whale' is used to indicate size rather than zoological affinity. This means that, in theory, a 'whale' is larger than a 'dolphin' and, in the same vein, a 'dolphin' is larger than a 'porpoise'. But there is so much overlap between these three groups that such a distinction is not as straightforward as it might sound – some whales are smaller than the largest dolphins, and some dolphins are smaller than the largest porpoises. The situation is even more complicated in North America, where every small member of the group is commonly referred to as a porpoise, wherever its true affinity lies.

Common names are notoriously confusing anywhere in the world. Some species have especially befuddling names: the rightwhale dolphins, for example, were named after right whales but are actually dolphins. At the same time, every species is known by umpteen different names in at least as many different languages. Thus the Yangtze river dolphin, beiji, pei c'hi, whitefin dolphin, whiteflag dolphin, Chinese river dolphin and baiji are all the same species. Even when almost everyone agrees on a name, there is still a certain amount of squabbling over the spelling, as in the bottlenose, bottlenosed and bottle-nose dolphin.

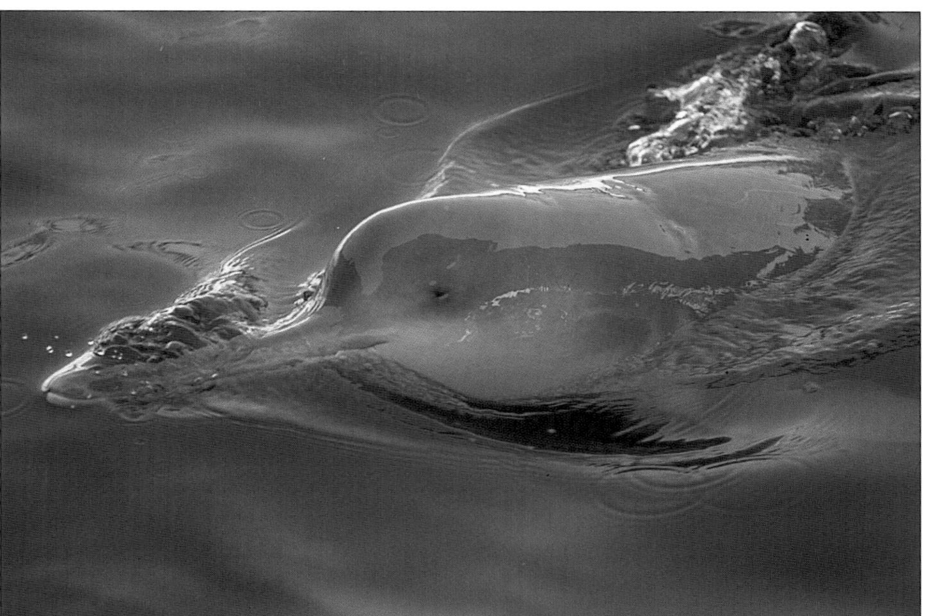

The river dolphins are superbly adapted to life in some of the largest, muddiest rivers in Asia and South America. This is a Yangtze river dolphin, or baiji, which lives only in the Yangtze River, China, and is probably the rarest of all the world's cetaceans, with fewer than 100 survivors.

To add to the confusion, six members of the dolphin family have the word 'whale' in their names: killer whale, long-finned pilot whale, short-finned pilot whale, melon-headed whale, pygmy killer whale and false killer whale. These are often grouped together as the 'blackfish', which is another confusing term, since not all of them are black and, of course, none of them are fish. The blackfish are considered by most experts to be more closely related to dolphins than to other whale species, and all thirty-three of them are usually placed together in the family Delphinidae. With this in mind, it could be argued that the killer whale would more appropriately be called the killer dolphin.

As if all this is not enough, there is even a 'dolphinfish', which is not a dolphin at all. It is actually a white-fleshed saltwater fish, otherwise known as the 'mahi-mahi'. Not surprisingly, its rather unfortunate name frequently causes consternation in restaurants frequented by dolphin devotees.

Fortunately, there is method in all this madness. Ignore the confusing and contradictory common names for a moment, and consider only the scientific ones. As with all officially recognized animals and plants, whales, dolphins and porpoises each have their own scientific name. This is based on Latin and is used by scientists throughout the world, whatever the language they speak. Since no species has more than one scientific name, and no two species have exactly the same scientific name, they can never be confused. For example, there are two different species of spotted dolphin, known in the scientific world as *Stenella attenuata* and *Stenella frontalis* respectively. When these scientific names are used, no matter what common names they may have, and in whatever language, the two species can never be mixed up.

A scientific name is written in italics, or underlined, and normally consists of two different words. These identify the animal, and also show which group it belongs to in the living world. The first word represents the genus, while the second defines the species. Biologists classify all living things by arranging them in groups, according to their similarities and differences. The smallest is a species, which is a group of living things that can breed together in the wild. A genus is simply a group of closely related species. In the same vein, a group of closely related genera (plural of genus) forms a family; then closely related families are grouped into orders, closely related orders into classes, and so on.

Take the two spotted dolphins as an example. They are officially classified in the following way:

Like many oceanic dolphins, the striped dolphin is an energetic animal and is often highly conspicuous.

	PANTROPICAL SPOTTED DOLPHIN:	ATLANTIC SPOTTED DOLPHIN:
Class:	Mammalia (mammals)	Mammalia (mammals)
Order:	Cetacea (cetaceans)	Cetacea (cetaceans)
Family:	Delphinidae (oceanic dolphins)	Delphinidae (oceanic dolphins)
Genus:	*Stenella*	*Stenella*
Species:	*attenuata*	*frontalis*

Since they are so closely related, and resemble one another in appearance, they are placed in the same genus. As it happens, the striped dolphin, short-snouted spinner dolphin and long-snouted spinner dolphin are also placed in the genus *Stenella*; although they are not covered in spots, they do share a number of other important features.

This is the theory of classification, and it works very well – most of the time. In practice, of course, scientific names and groupings occasionally have to be changed as new information comes to light, or when biologists disagree over the details of a particular grouping. It is also necessary, in some cases, to add extra groupings to the system – sub-orders, sub-families and sub-species – in order to deal with more complex relationships.

Eighty species are currently recognized in the order Cetacea (which comes from the Latin *cetus*, meaning a large sea animal, and the Greek *ketos*, meaning a sea monster). Known collectively as cetaceans, they include all the world's whales, dolphins and porpoises. Since they do not fit neatly into three groups with these particular names, they are divided into two living sub-orders: the Odontoceti and the Mysticeti. There is also a third sub-order of extinct species, or ancient whales, known as the Archaeoceti.

The mysticetes, or baleen whales, are distinctive because they do not have teeth. Instead, they have hundreds of special comb-like baleen plates, or 'whalebones', hanging down from their upper jaws. These plates overlap inside their mouths and have stiff hairs, which form sieves to filter food out of the sea water. Their vast jaws enable them to catch thousands of shrimp-like crustaceans or small fish in one gulp. This group includes most of the larger whales, such as the blue, grey and humpback. There are four families altogether.

The odontocetes, or toothed whales, are distinctive because they do have teeth. They feed mostly on fish, squid and, in a few cases, marine mammals,

Despite its name, the short-finned pilot whale is a member of the family Delphinidae and is therefore, strictly speaking, a dolphin.

and normally capture one animal at a time. This group includes all the oceanic dolphins and blackfish, as well as the narwhal and beluga, porpoises, river dolphins, sperm whales and beaked whales. There are nine families altogether. Many of them are very distinctive, but the classification of oceanic dolphins, blackfish, river dolphins and porpoises requires a little more explanation.

There are six species of porpoise, all belonging to one family – the Phocoenidae. They are typically more robust than dolphins, have rounded foreheads and no beaks, tend to show little of themselves at the surface, and live mainly (but not exclusively) along the coast. But their teeth are their most distinctive feature, being spade-shaped (in dolphins, they are conical).

The river dolphins live in some of the largest, muddiest rivers in Asia and South America. Their collective name is rather confusing, because they are not exclusively riverine animals (the franciscana prefers shallow coastal waters), nor are they the only cetaceans living in rivers (tucuxis, finless porpoises and several other species regularly inhabit freshwater). They are not closely related to oceanic dolphins, despite the obvious similarities in their appearance, and the two groups seem to have evolved quite separately. Most river dolphins are fairly small animals, with noticeably long, narrow beaks and large numbers of pointed teeth, poorly developed dorsal fins, and such tiny eyes that they are almost blind. There are five species altogether, divided into three different families.

The blackfish, or smaller-toothed whales, form an interestingly varied group. In size alone, they range from as little as 2.1 metres (7 feet) long in the pygmy killer whale to a maximum of 9.8 metres (32 feet) in the male killer whale. They are gregarious by nature, preferring to live in well-structured groups, and frequently associate with oceanic dolphins. However, since they are unlike most dolphins in appearance, and because they are popularly viewed as whales, they are not included in this book.

WHALE, DOLPHIN AND PORPOISE FAMILIES

BALEEN WHALES:

Balaenidae
Right whales and Bowhead whale ....3 species
Neobalaenidae
Pygmy right whale......................1 species
Eschrichtiidae
Grey whale.................................1 species
Balaenopteridae
Rorqual whales ....6 species

TOOTHED WHALES:

Kogiidae
Pygmy and Dwarf sperm whales......................................2 species
Physeteridae
Sperm whale ....1 species
Monodontidae
Narwhal and Beluga ....2 species
Ziphiidae
Beaked whales ....20 species
Delphinidae
Blackfish and Oceanic dolphins...................................33 species
Iniidae
Amazon river dolphin.................1 species
Pontoporiidae
Yangtze river dolphin and Franciscana ....2 species
Platanistidae
Indus and Ganges river dolphins ....2 species
Phocoenidae
Porpoises ....6 species

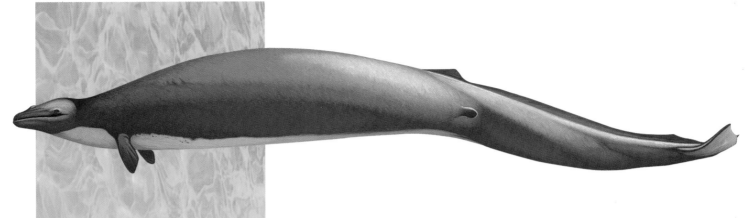

Cetaceans probably evolved from furry land mammals with four legs. The first real whale- or dolphin-like animals, called Archaeocetes, appeared about 50 million years ago.

When watching dolphins, it is impossible not to marvel at their complete mastery of the underwater world.

The Evolution of Dolphins

The Earth has existed for about 4.5 billion years, and the first forms of life appeared about 700,000 million years later. These were tiny, simple cells that are believed to have originated in the 'primeval soup' – the chemical-rich seawater formed during the planet's early history.

Simple plants and animals later began to emerge and, over billions of years, innumerable life forms flourished and disappeared. But they all lived in the sea. It was not until 400–500 million years ago – a relatively short time in the history of the planet – that the first plants and animals ventured out of the water and onto dry land.

It was on land that the world's first mammals are believed to have appeared. Roughly the size and shape of modern shrews, they probably evolved from

mammal-like reptiles a little under 200 million years ago. For the first two-thirds of their subsequent history, these early mammals remained small and inconspicuous. Then their luck changed dramatically. With the mass extinction of the dinosaurs, about 65 million years ago, a profusion of niches were opened up for exploitation. Mammals large and small flourished and diversified as they adapted to take advantage of all the new opportunities suddenly open to them.

Exactly how, or why, some of these mammals returned to the sea is still unclear. Most experts believe that modern cetaceans evolved from land-based hoofed mammals, which lived around brackish estuaries and lagoons about 55–65 million years ago. Known as mesonychids, these strange animals were widely distributed, and ranged in size from something like a small dog to a large bear. They are believed to have given rise to ancient whales, as well as to modern hoofed mammals.

Gradually, the mesonychids spent more and more time in the water, foraging for fish and other aquatic animals. But their new ocean home presented some daunting challenges for air-breathing four-legged mammals – and they had to evolve to survive. They became more streamlined; they began to replace the traditional mammalian hair with insulating blubber; their nostrils moved towards the tops of their heads to make breathing at the surface easier; they developed stronger tails for swimming; their front limbs began to turn into paddles; and their back limbs slowly wasted away.

The evidence from the fossil record shows that the speed and magnitude of these transformations were nothing short of remarkable. This was probably because, while the sea was fundamentally hostile to early cetaceans and their ancestors, it also offered some outstanding opportunities. Fish and

The English word 'dolphin' is believed to come from the Greek word delphys, *which means 'womb'; this is a symbol for the source of life, illustrating the importance attached to dolphins since early times.*

invertebrates were available in abundance and, at least initially, there was likely to have been little competition from other predators.

The first recognizable cetaceans appeared about fifty million years ago. Known as the archaeocetes, or ancient whales, they were not the direct ancestors of modern cetaceans but were probably very similar. Ranging in length from about 2 metres (6 feet 6 inches) to 21 metres (69 feet), they lived mainly in coastal swamps and shallow seas. They died out after approximately twenty million years – a good innings for most species.

By the time the archaeocetes had gone, a wide variety of cetaceans ranged across the world's oceans. None of them were quite the same as modern whales and dolphins, but their general body form, way of life and dentition were unmistakably similar. They had also diverged, probably from the same ancestor, into the two distinct groups we know today: the Odontocetes (dolphins and other toothed species) and the Mysticetes (baleen or whalebone whales). Dolphins resembling modern species, and representatives of families around today, first appeared less than fifteen million years ago.

Despite this logical evolutionary progression, it is doubtless hard to imagine how four-legged, furry animals standing at the water's edge were able to evolve into sleek, flippered, fluked, almost hairless creatures swimming in the sea. In fact, modern cetaceans now bear so little obvious resemblance to their terrestrial ancestors that they are helpless, and extremely vulnerable, out of

Dolphins have shed most external traces of their terrestrial ancestry and are supremely adapted to underwater life. Their body shape has become streamlined, they have lost most of their body hair, their front limbs have turned into flippers, their hind limbs have disappeared, and their muscular tails provide a powerful means of propulsion.

water. It is the price they have to pay for their complete mastery of the underwater world. But they still carry in their bodies some of the physical traits of their land-dwelling ancestors. Perhaps the best example is the bone structure of the dolphin flipper, which closely resembles an arm and hand with fingers; further evidence is provided by the remains of pelvic bones that millions of years ago held their hind limbs.

Unfortunately, though, the fossil record is far from complete and there are huge gaps in our knowledge spanning many millions of years. There is good evidence to suggest that the transition to an aquatic way of life occurred around the ancient Tethys Sea (which subsequently divided, as the continents moved, to form what is now the Mediterranean Sea and the north-western Indian Ocean) but many of the details are left to sophisticated guesswork. Tiny fragments – a few teeth or minuscule pieces of bone – sometimes provide the only tantalising glimpse of an important link in the evolutionary chain. Even then, it often takes years of careful analysis and research to identify each find – and, of course, later discoveries may throw all the conclusions into question.

One thing we do know is that, in the history of cetaceans, hundreds or even thousands of species and families have been and gone. Sadly, we evolved much too late to see the majority of them, although there are believed to be at least as many species alive today as there have been at any time in the past.

CHAPTER

2

Dolphin Design

Humans have broken a string of remarkable records in terms of depth-diving, breath-hold diving, speed-swimming and long-distance swimming. But even the world's best divers and swimmers would be poor competition for a dolphin. The reason is simple: millions of years of evolution have designed the dolphin's body to make it supremely adapted to life beneath the ocean waves.

Bottlenose dolphin, The Bahamas.

Is it a Mammal? Or a Fish?

Dolphins are mammals: they are warm-blooded; they breathe air with lungs; and they suckle their young using milk from the female's mammary glands. In contrast, fish are cold-blooded; they extract all the oxygen they need directly from the water, with the help of gills; and most of them either lay eggs or give birth to independently feeding young.

But over the centuries, people have repeatedly mistaken dolphins for fish. Even today, they are commonly regarded as 'spouting fish' or 'fish with lungs' and, as a result, are treated with as little respect as any other fish by coastal communities in many parts of the world.

In some ways, this is understandable. Dolphins have shed most external traces of their terrestrial ancestry, and have lost many of the more obvious features normally associated with mammals. Their hair, for example, has all but disappeared (it is present only as sparse stubble in some new-born calves) and they do not have the familiar external ears of most of their land-based relatives. In short, they have become so streamlined, and so well adapted to life in an underwater world, that their bodies have evolved to become more fish-like than mammal-like in appearance. However, this is as far as the comparison goes; dolphins are no more closely related to fish than we are. Their similarities are simply the result of convergent evolution in unrelated groups of animals, as they adapt to identical living conditions.

At first glance, dolphins closely resemble fish. Both the tucuxi and the Caribbean reef shark shown here, for example, have remarkably similar body shapes and both have dorsal fins, flippers and huge tails. In fact, the similarities are so striking that, for many years, dolphins and all other cetaceans were incorrectly believed to be 'spouting fish'.

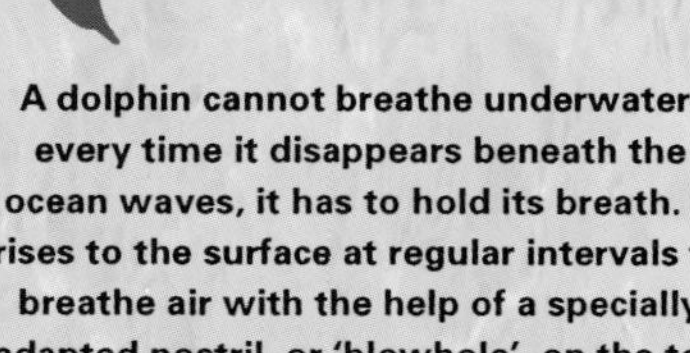

A dolphin cannot breathe underwater: every time it disappears beneath the ocean waves, it has to hold its breath. It rises to the surface at regular intervals to breathe air with the help of a specially adapted nostril, or 'blowhole', on the top of the head.

Dolphins have just a single dorsal fin, and even this is absent in the northern and southern rightwhale dolphins. Most fish, however, have more than one fin: the Caribbean reef shark below, for example, has a total of four.

A dolphin swims with the help of powerful muscles in the rear third of its body, which force the tail up and down to propel the animal through the water.

Both fish and dolphins have flippers, or pectoral fins. Shaped like paddles, these modified front limbs are used primarily for twisting and turning and for manoeuvring. Flipper sizes, shapes, and colours vary considerably from one species of dolphin to another.

A fish swims by moving its head from side to side, which sends 'waves' down its body. These increase in intensity and finally reach the tail, which then swings from side to side and propels the animal through the water.

Fish do not need to rise to the surface to breathe: with the help of their gills, they can take all the oxygen they need directly from the water.

A shark is covered in thousands of rough, tooth-like scales, but a dolphin's skin is velvety smooth to touch.

The blowhole can be opened and closed with the help of a special muscular plug, allowing the dolphin to keep water out of its lungs when diving.

How Does a Dolphin Breathe?

Like other mammals, dolphins need air to survive. This means that they cannot stay underwater indefinitely, and have to rise to the surface at frequent intervals to breathe. They hold their breath when they dive, and then return to the surface to expel the used air and replenish their lungs with fresh air before diving again.

They are unable to breathe through their mouths (because the trachea and oesophagus are separate) but they have a nostril, or 'blowhole', on the top of the head. Dolphins and all other toothed whales have a single blowhole, although its exact shape and position vary between species; in contrast, all the baleen whales have two blowholes side by side. The lungs are emptied and refilled through this blowhole: it opens, an explosive exhalation is followed immediately by an inhalation, and then it closes again. Powerful muscles form a special plug within the blowhole, preventing water from entering the lungs when the dolphin is underwater.

The breathing sequence often takes a mere fraction of a second. Since the blowhole is on the top of the head, only a small part of the head region and back needs to break the surface for the dolphin to be able to snatch a breath of air. Like an Olympic swimmer, it often begins to exhale just before reaching the surface, helping to cut the amount of time spent breathing still further. Most dolphins are able to snatch a breath five or six times in a minute before diving again, and since they normally keep swimming between (and during) surfacings their progress is hardly impeded.

The used air in the lungs is exhaled in a cloud of spray, known as a 'blow' or 'spout', although this is not as visible in dolphins as it is in many of the larger whales. Unlike humans, they do not have an automatic breathing reflex, which means that their breathing is under voluntary control. If they lose consciousness for any reason (in the way that we do when we are sleeping or under an anaesthetic) they would drown or suffocate. However, they breathe far less frequently than humans, compensating by taking deeper breaths and extracting oxygen from the air more efficiently, and with the help of a variety of physiological adaptations (see Chapter 4).

Like Olympic swimmers, dolphins often exhale just before they reach the surface, helping to reduce the amount of time spent above water to just a fraction of a second.

Dolphins as Marine Mammals

Millions of years ago, many mammals made their home in the sea. It has even been suggested that early human ancestors followed this well-trodden path and did an evolutionary stint in lagoons and shallow coastal waters – perhaps accounting for our shortage of hair and upright stance. If this 'aquatic ape theory' is to be believed, our ancestors returned to their former terrestrial lifestyle while certain other mammalian groups never looked back. Three of these survive today: the cetaceans (whales, dolphins and porpoises); the sirenians (sea cows); and the pinnipeds (seals, sealions and walrus). They are not closely related groups, and differ in the degrees to which they are adapted to life underwater, but they do show some interesting similarities and differences.

Strictly speaking, not all members of these groups are genuinely marine. The Baikal seal, the Amazonian manatee and four species of river dolphins are confined to freshwater, while a number of others split their time between saltwater, brackish and freshwater environments. But the majority of them do live exclusively in the sea.

The sirenians, or sea cows, include only four living species: the dugong and the West Indian, Amazonian and West African manatees. A fifth species, Steller's sea cow, became extinct late in the 18th century and has the unhappy distinction of being one of only two marine mammals to have disappeared in modern times (the other being the recently extinct Caribbean monk seal). The sea cows are the only mammals other than cetaceans to be exclusively aquatic. They complete their entire life cycle in water. Superficially similar to dolphins

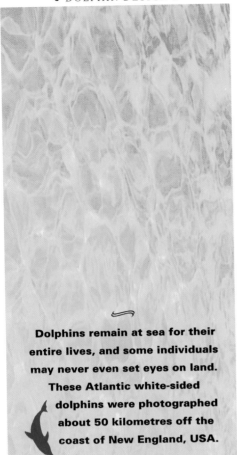

Dolphins remain at sea for their entire lives, and some individuals may never even set eyes on land. These Atlantic white-sided dolphins were photographed about 50 kilometres off the coast of New England, USA.

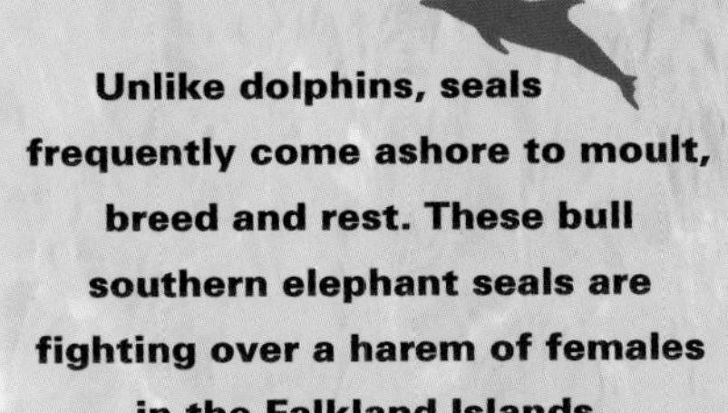

Unlike dolphins, seals frequently come ashore to moult, breed and rest. These bull southern elephant seals are fighting over a harem of females in the Falkland Islands.

and other cetaceans, they have a horizontal tail, no external hind limbs, paddle-like front flippers and a cylindrical body. Their nearest living relatives are believed to include elephants and, possibly, hyraxes.

The pinnipeds, or seals, sealions and walrus, consists of thirty-three living species (excluding the Caribbean monk seal, which was last seen in 1952). They are all amphibious. Although they are all powerful swimmers, and are superbly adapted to life in the sea, they have not made a total break from the land. All their feeding is done in the sea but, unlike cetaceans and sea cows, they have to come ashore (or, in some cases, onto ice) to moult, rest and breed. They also frequently seek refuge on land from sea-based predators and other dangers. Pinnipeds have four webbed limbs armed with claws at the ends of all the digits (they have not lost their hind limbs); they have several different types of teeth for cutting and chewing (cetaceans and sea cows normally have rows of identical teeth); and most have a dense coat of fur. Their nearest living relatives are believed to include bears, cats, dogs and other carnivores.

Several other mammals also make their home in the sea although, within their groups, they are the exceptions rather than the rules. The sea otter makes its living in the sea and is extremely well adapted to marine life; it comes ashore occasionally in some areas, but normally gives birth, cares for its young, mates, moults and forages in the water. The marine otter, which is found mainly along rocky, exposed coasts, also deserves a mention: although it spends much of its time on land, it forages in the sea. Finally, the polar bear spends much of its life at sea, usually on ice, although the females den and give birth on land.

During the course of evolution, major changes have taken place in the bodies of dolphins to equip them for life underwater. Many of their more obvious adaptations are shown here and opposite.

Anatomy of a Dolphin

Almost everything about the dolphin's anatomy has something to do with its underwater life. Its body is streamlined and has lost most of its body hair, to improve hydrodynamic efficiency; it has a short, stiff neck, which is essential for swimming at high speed; its front limbs have turned into flippers and its hind limbs have disappeared; it has a muscular tail to provide a powerful means of propulsion; and its nostrils have moved to the top of the head for easy breathing at the surface. Many other, perhaps less obvious, adaptations help it to thrive in what might otherwise be considered (for a mammal at least) an alien world.

Land mammals come in a multitude of shapes, from long and thin to short and fat, and have all manner of limbs and other protuberances sticking out of their bodies. This causes few problems, because they move around in air. But travelling in water is much harder work and dolphins need streamlined bodies to minimise the amount of effort required for swimming. They are torpedo-shaped – their bodies are larger at the front than at the back – and all their protruding parts, which would otherwise slow them down, are reduced or tucked away. This is one reason why the penis of the male is completely hidden within muscular folds, and the teats of the female are concealed within slits on either side of the genital area.

They have also lost any trace of the fur that was almost certainly present on their early ancestors. Fur would slow them down in the water as much as a poorly streamlined body. Although new-born calves sometimes have a small amount of stubble on their beaks, dolphins have extremely smooth, velvety skin, which helps them to slip through the water with apparent ease.

However, like all mammals, dolphins are warm-blooded. They need to maintain a stable body temperature of around 36–37°C. This is particularly difficult in water, which is an excellent conductor of heat and sucks it out of a typical mammal up to twenty-five times faster than air. Most mammals rely on

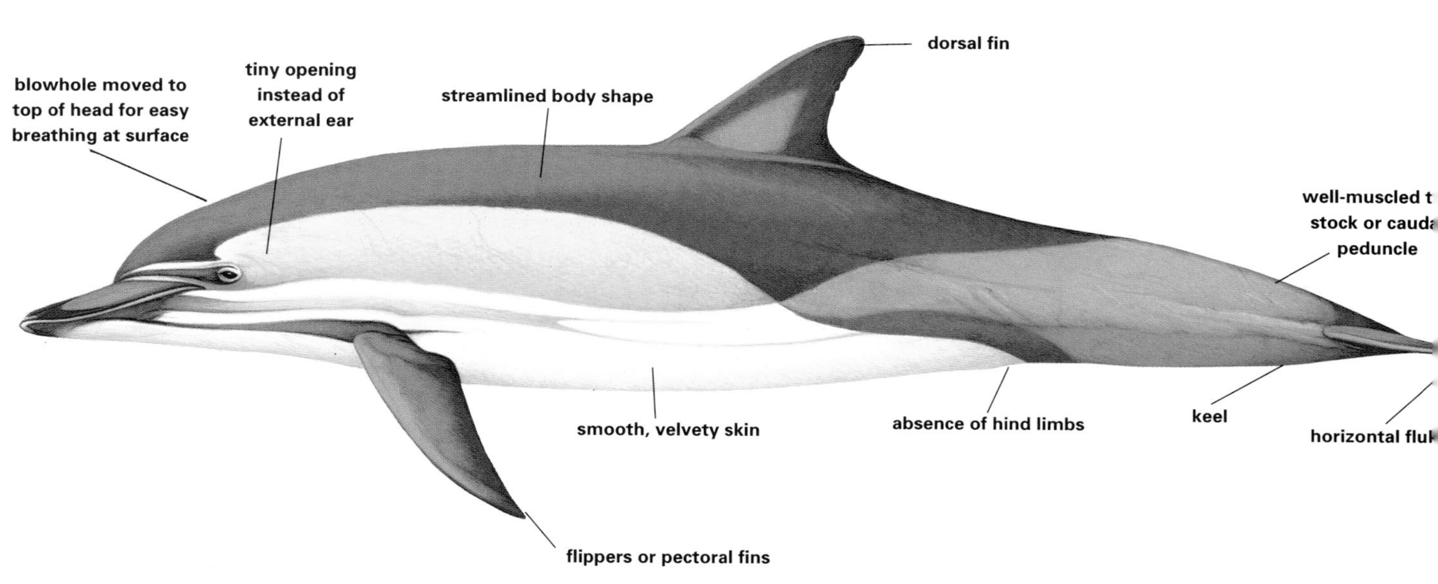

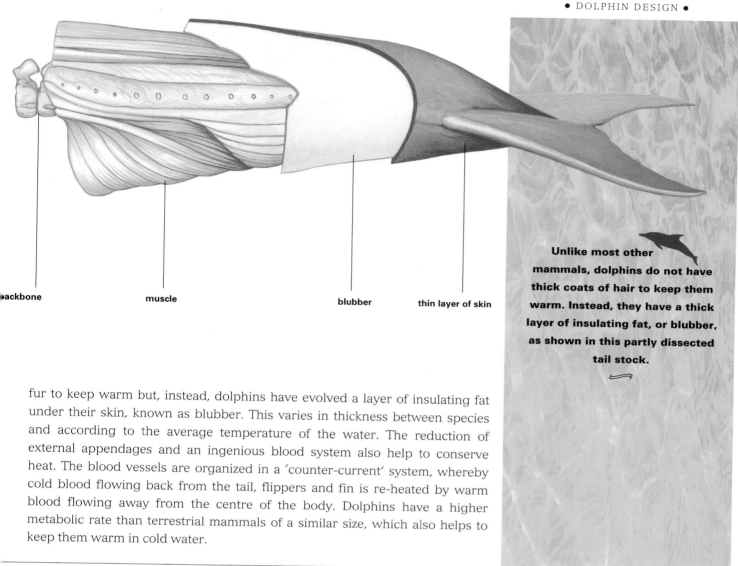

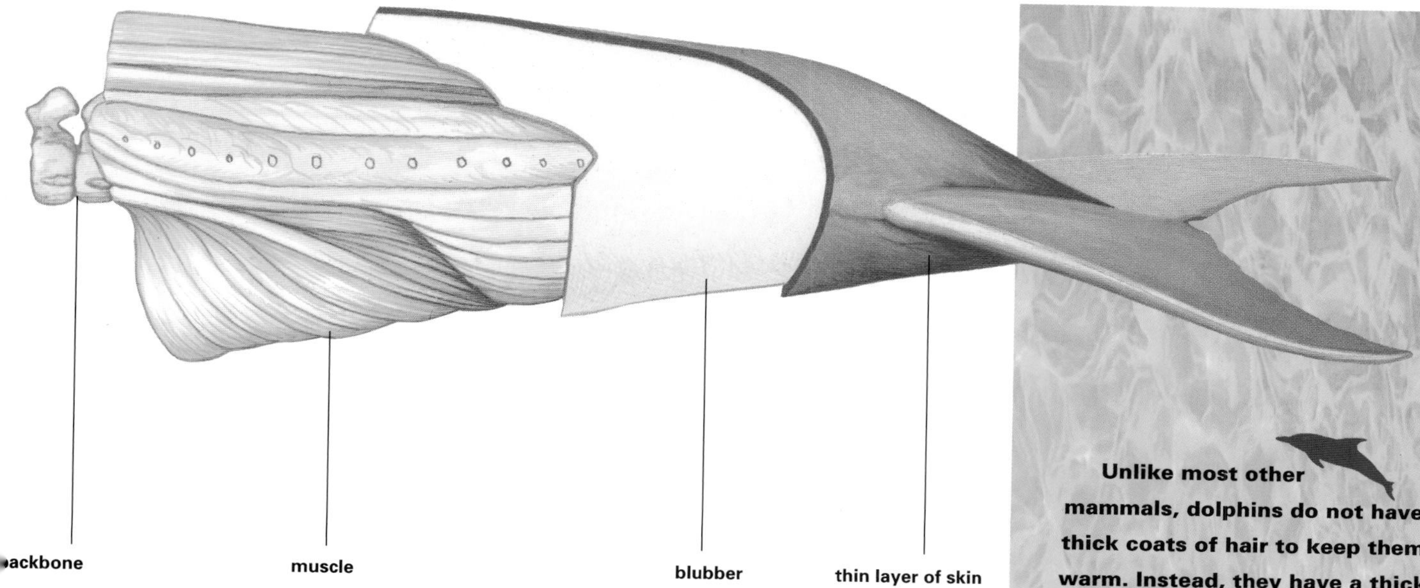

ackbone

muscle

blubber

thin layer of skin

Unlike most other mammals, dolphins do not have thick coats of hair to keep them warm. Instead, they have a thick layer of insulating fat, or blubber, as shown in this partly dissected tail stock.

fur to keep warm but, instead, dolphins have evolved a layer of insulating fat under their skin, known as blubber. This varies in thickness between species and according to the average temperature of the water. The reduction of external appendages and an ingenious blood system also help to conserve heat. The blood vessels are organized in a 'counter-current' system, whereby cold blood flowing back from the tail, flippers and fin is re-heated by warm blood flowing away from the centre of the body. Dolphins have a higher metabolic rate than terrestrial mammals of a similar size, which also helps to keep them warm in cold water.

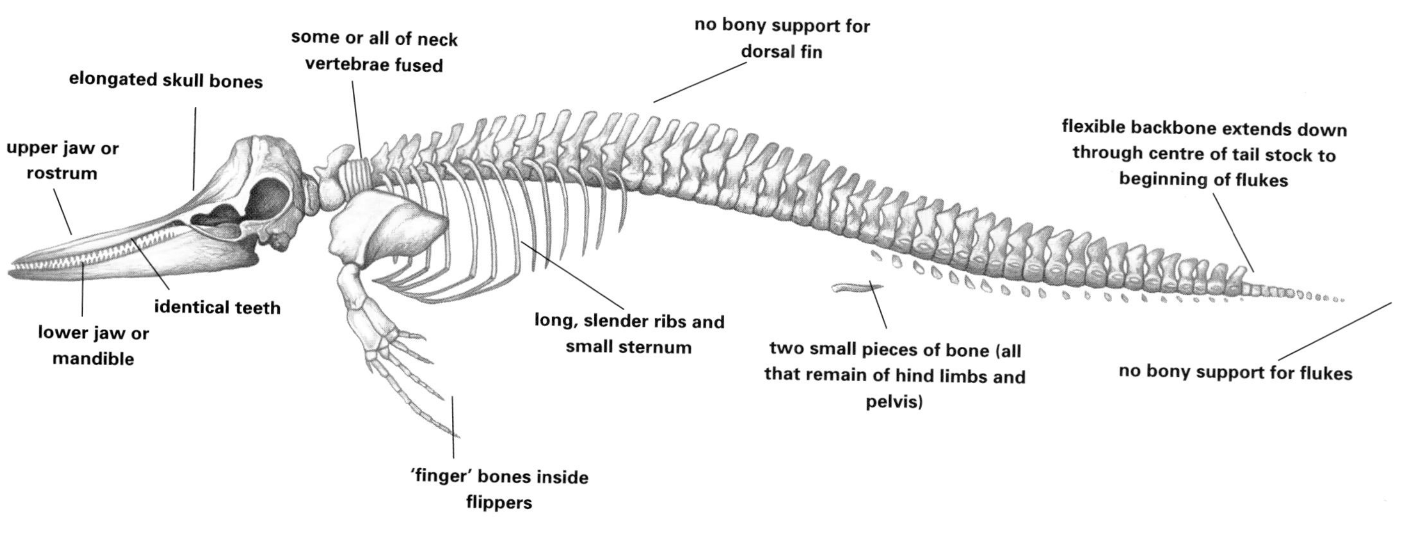

Teeth and Bones Dolphin skeletons are weaker than those of land mammals of a similar size: thanks to the buoyancy of the water, they do not need strong limbs for support. The skull is remarkable for the great elongation of its face bones, known as 'telescoping', which means that both the upper and lower jaws are unusually long. The backbone is very flexible, due to the reduced interlocking of individual vertebrae and the development of large fibrous discs between them, to allow powerful undulations of the tail for swimming. The seven neck vertebrae (found in nearly all mammals) have become greatly compressed and, in some places, fused. This makes the neck short and stiff, and is an essential adaptation for swimming at high speed; however, it means that most dolphins are unable to move their heads much from side to side, and can do little more than nod up and down.

The teeth are particularly interesting, and differ from other mammals in a number of ways. All dolphins have teeth, although the number varies greatly from species to species. At one extreme, long-snouted spinner dolphins have as many as 252 small, sharp teeth in their long, narrow jaws; this is more than any other mammal. At the other extreme, Risso's dolphins have no upper teeth and only four to fourteen lower teeth in their short, broad jaws. It is unusual among mammals for all the teeth to be identical, but this is the case in oceanic dolphins: they are not differentiated into incisors, canines, pre-molars and molars. They are all conical, which is an ideal shape for grasping rapidly moving, slippery prey. There are few major variations within this theme, although the rough-toothed dolphin has developed wrinkled enamel and Risso's dolphin has slightly chunkier, oval teeth than the other species. Interestingly, while most mammals have two sets of teeth, dolphins retain their first teeth (the 'baby' or 'milk' teeth) throughout their lives; these begin to form before birth and erupt when the calf is a few weeks old.

The front limbs have been reduced to minimise resistance in the water and have evolved into flippers. It is still possible to see the typical structure of the mammalian hand in the skeleton. The fingers have spread out and lengthened, thus increasing the surface area, and the rigidity is enhanced by the fact that the only mobile joint is the shoulder. Flippers provide excellent paddles for steering and stability, but they also appear to be important as organs of touch in social and sexual contexts. The hind limbs have all but disappeared: there are still traces of the pelvic girdle and, in some cases, the femur buried deep inside the abdominal blubber and muscle.

The dorsal fin is particularly interesting because it is not related to any other typically mammalian structure. Sometimes the only part of a dolphin seen in the wild, it contains no bones but is made of a tough, fibrous fatty material. It has two likely functions, although these may not be essential because some species have very small fins and, indeed, the two rightwhale dolphins have no fins at all. It may serve for balance, acting like the keel on a sailing boat to stabilise the animal as it speeds through the water. It may also help with temperature regulation, acting as a heat exchanger during intense activity or when swimming in particularly warm water.

Like the dorsal fin, the flukes are boneless and made of a tough, fibrous fatty material. They feel rather like dense rubber to touch. Attached to the end of the spine, they are always horizontal and form a perfect hydrofoil, like an aircraft wing in cross-section. When a dolphin swims, the massive muscles in the rear half of the body, known as the 'tail stock', move the flukes up and down. The upward motion is the power stroke, the downward motion the recovery stroke.

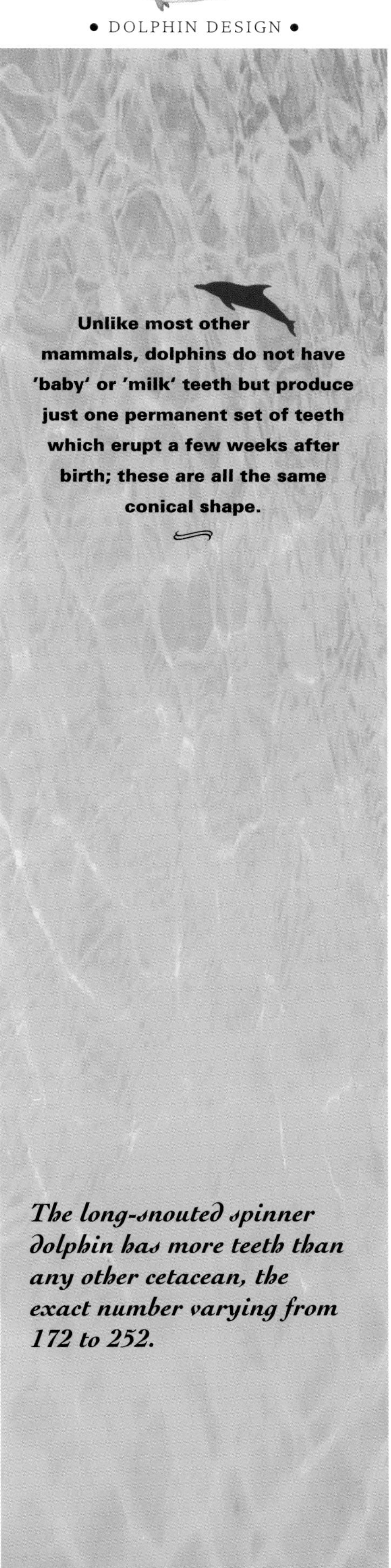

Unlike most other mammals, dolphins do not have 'baby' or 'milk' teeth but produce just one permanent set of teeth which erupt a few weeks after birth; these are all the same conical shape.

The long-snouted spinner dolphin has more teeth than any other cetacean, the exact number varying from 172 to 252.

CHAPTER

3

Sensing the Environment

Dolphins perceive the world in ways that are well beyond the scope of our own senses. Whereas we rely mainly on sight and hearing, and retain the senses of touch, taste and smell, they have had to adapt in different ways to suit their aquatic environment. Sight and touch are important to them, and they retain the sense of taste, but their primary source of information is hearing – which they have developed to an extraordinary degree. They are also believed to have a little-known sixth sense, enabling them to detect geomagnetism and then use it like an unseen map to find their way around.

Common dolphin, California, USA.

Sight, Hearing, Touch, Taste and Smell

Sight Human eyes are specifically adapted for focusing in air and, consequently, if we try to see underwater, everything looks blurred. The only way we can overcome this problem is by wearing tightly fitting goggles, which trap air around our eyes and enable us to look through glass 'windows'. Dolphins have overcome this problem by means of physiological change, and are able to see in both air and water. Most dolphins can see very well, although visual acuity probably varies from one species to another, and they are also able to discriminate fine details. There is still some controversy over the precise means by which they can see both above and below the surface, but it probably has something to do with the great elasticity of their eye lenses.

Highly sensitive nerve endings around the blowhole are believed to help a dolphin recognize the exact moment when the top of its head breaks the surface of the water.

Nevertheless, sight is of limited benefit to dolphins, and they rely on their eyes less than most terrestrial mammals. The problem is that water is much less transparent to light than air. Some light is reflected off the surface; some is scattered by particles underwater; and some is absorbed by the water itself. So, the deeper the water, the darker it gets. Even in crystal clear seas, as much as 90 per cent of the light is lost at a depth of only 10 metres (33 feet), and this increases to 99 per cent at a depth of 40 metres (132 feet). Many dolphins therefore spend a substantial proportion of their lives in pitch darkness.

It does not simply get darker with depth, because the light is not absorbed uniformly. Sunlight is composed of various colours mixed together, which disappear, one by one, as depth increases. Red is absorbed first, followed by orange, then yellow, green and ultimately blue. All the colours can be seen in shallow water, but in water deeper than a few metres everything tends to appear blue-green. It is believed that some dolphins, at least, may be able to see in colour. Their eyes certainly have cone-like receptors, which are essential for sensing different wavelengths of light in order to see colours. But little is known about their abilities in this area, and the limited evidence available is rather contradictory. Wild dolphins sometimes show a strong preference for red and yellow objects, for example, and yet trials with captive dolphins have so far had little success in teaching them to distinguish between different colours.

Hearing The problems associated with sight underwater, and the many advantages of using sound instead, have shaped the way dolphins sense the outside world. Sound travels through water nearly five times faster than through air (1,500 metres per second compared with 330 metres per second) and can be heard over much longer distances below the surface. It is not surprising that dolphins have highly developed hearing abilities and that a large proportion of their brains are devoted to the analysis of sounds. They can hear a wide range of frequencies and are able to determine the direction of different sound sources with pinpoint accuracy.

But it is hard to imagine how they can have such acute hearing when they have no visible ears. Humans and other land mammals have distinctive outer ears – flaps of cartilage used to funnel sound waves towards the ear drums – but these are completely absent in dolphins. During the course of evolution, they have been sacrificed for the sake of a streamlined body. Instead, there is a tiny hole in the skin, a few centimetres behind each eye, which leads to the inner ear.

However, there is considerable disagreement over the path by which the dolphin inner ear receives sound. Some experts claim that the ear hole and the auditory meatus (the water-filled channel between the outside of the head and the ear structure) have become as redundant as the human appendix. There is, indeed, a second sound-receiving organ – the lower jaw. This contains oil-filled sinuses that are believed to be able to channel sound waves directly to the inner ear. It is quite possible, of course, that both the ear and the lower jaw are used for hearing – the ear for receiving atmospheric and communication sounds, the lower jaw for echolocation clicks, for example.

There is another important hearing adaptation that enables dolphins to identify the direction of different sound sources underwater. Humans have the

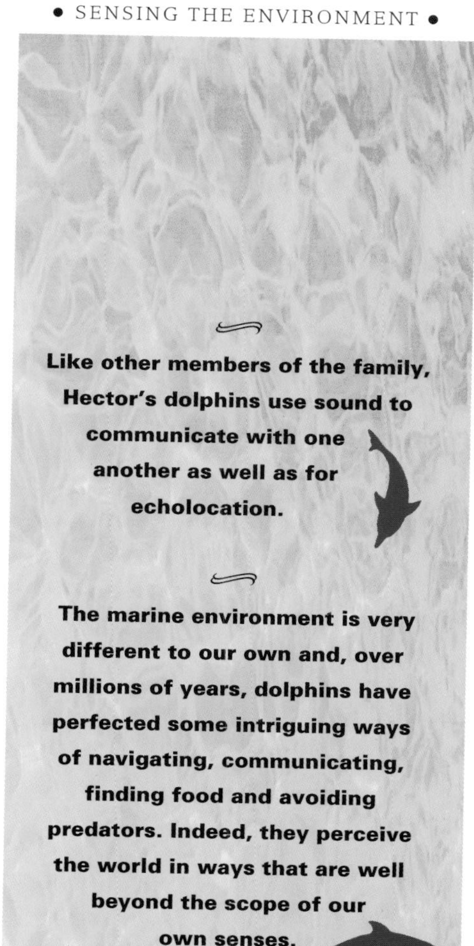

Like other members of the family, Hector's dolphins use sound to communicate with one another as well as for echolocation.

The marine environment is very different to our own and, over millions of years, dolphins have perfected some intriguing ways of navigating, communicating, finding food and avoiding predators. Indeed, they perceive the world in ways that are well beyond the scope of our own senses.

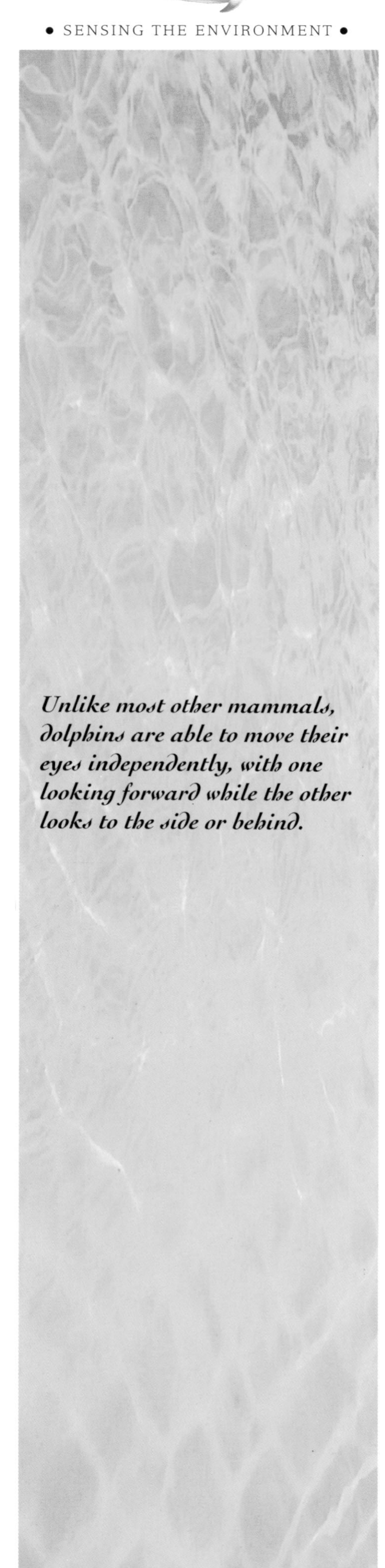

Unlike most other mammals, dolphins are able to move their eyes independently, with one looking forward while the other looks to the side or behind.

same ability in air, but as soon as we put our heads in water we find it impossible to tell where even the loudest sounds are coming from. This is because sound is reflected off a mammalian head in air (meaning that the side of the head nearest the source receives a stronger signal than the other side) but it travels straight through the head underwater. Dolphins have solved the problem with the help of a radical adaptation to their inner ear. The hearing apparatus is acoustically isolated from the skull by foam-filled air spaces, whereas in terrestrial mammals it is actually embedded in the bones of the skull. These air spaces are believed to insulate the inner ear from extraneous sound passing through the head. This helps to explain how a dolphin's hearing can be highly directional. It is believed to be a highly efficient system that works even under a pressure of 100 atmospheres (equivalent to a water depth of 1,000 metres or 3,280 feet).

Touch Touch is also an important sense for dolphins, both for investigating unfamiliar objects and in a social context (they frequently touch one another as a form of greeting and, perhaps, to strengthen social bonds). However, although their sense of touch is highly developed, its potential is fairly limited. Humans have grasping hands and fingers to obtain information on the weight, texture and three-dimensional shape of objects, but as dolphins have had a greater need for a more streamlined body, they have been left without such manipulative limbs. Nevertheless, they are able to use their flippers to a certain degree, as well as their dorsal fin, beak and skin. Males even use their penises – not just in a sexual context, but also to investigate the details of their immediate environment.

Dolphin skin is easily damaged, and is so thin that a sharp fingernail could draw blood; although their wounds heal very quickly, many individuals are heavily scarred by the time they reach old age. Their skin is highly sensitive to touch, and will elicit a reaction even to something as delicate as the stroke of a feather. Some parts of the skin have more nerve endings than others, and are therefore especially sensitive. The skin around the blowhole, in particular, may be able to detect when the top of the head is clear of the water and therefore when it is safe to breathe. As any snorkeller will know, it can be extremely difficult to judge the precise moment when the top of the head – let alone the snorkel – is in the air. Yet, in calm sea conditions, dolphins frequently start to blow air from their lungs while they are still underwater, and then take a breath the moment the blowhole clears the surface. Another special function of the skin may be to sense the first signs of turbulence in water flow over the body, and then to counteract it. Some species may also be able to sense pressure build-up in the jaw region, and thus tell how fast they are swimming.

Taste and Smell Taste and smell are both senses for detecting chemicals. On land, there is a clear distinction between the two – taste detects chemicals in solution, and smell detects them in the air. Underwater, even though the transfer of chemical information can occur only in solution, it is still possible to smell. The distinction is just a little more subtle: taste is used for objects in or near the mouth, while smell is important over longer distances.

Sharks, for example, have an excellent sense of smell, and can pick up the scent of blood and other body fluids from huge distances. Their nostrils are packed with cells that detect odours but, of course, they are not used for breathing air.

Dolphins, on the other hand, have lost their sense of smell. This is simply for logistical reasons: their nostrils have to be closed underwater (otherwise they would drown), and they spend only a short time surfacing for air. However, they have retained a sense of taste. The region of the brain associated with taste is well developed, and they have special pits that appear to be taste

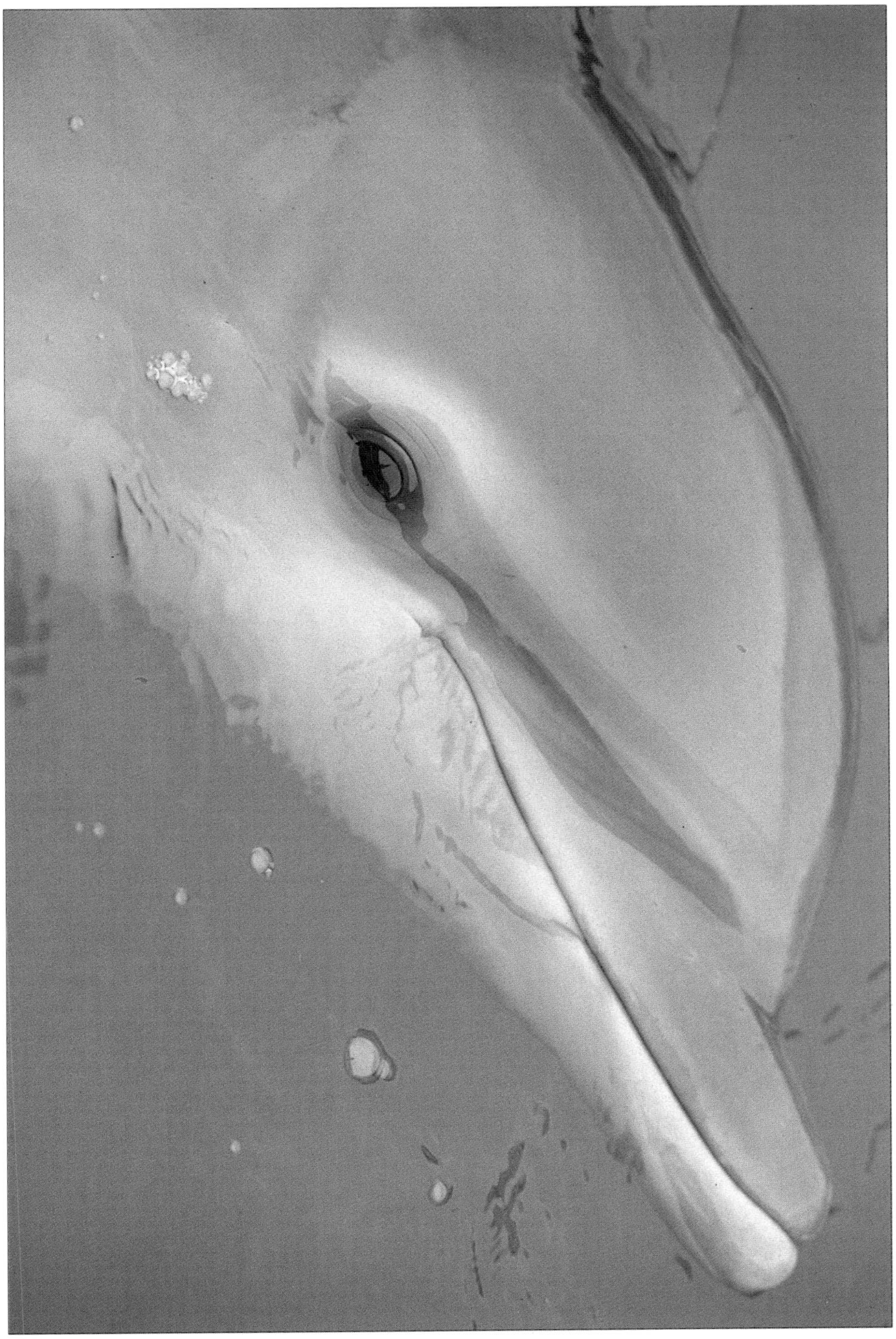

It is believed that dolphins have fairly good eyesight both above and below the water; this is probably because of the great elasticity of their eye lenses, which can adapt according to requirements.

receptors at the base of the tongue. Studies on dolphins in captivity reveal that they are able to discriminate between different chemicals, but they do not appear to respond in the same way as humans to the sensations of sour, bitter, salty and sweet; chemicals that we find bitter and distasteful, for example, do not seem to bother dolphins at all.

Taste could have several possible functions underwater. Since dolphins can probably pick up chemicals from both inside and outside the mouth, it may even perform the normal function of smell to some extent as well – although it certainly would not compare with the olfactory system in sharks. In a social context, it may be used to detect changes in the urine or faeces of other dolphins; these may contain sexual pheromones that would indicate a readiness to mate, and they may even provide trails to follow during long-distance migrations. Alternatively, it may be used to test food, for example for signs of decomposition, or to gain a range of other information on the local environment.

Echolocation: Seeing with Sound

Dolphins are able to build up a 'picture' of their surroundings with the help of sound. They use a remarkable sensory system, called echolocation, which has evolved independently in a number of animals that hunt fast-moving prey in darkness: dolphins, bats, some shrews, oilbirds and cave swiftlets among them.

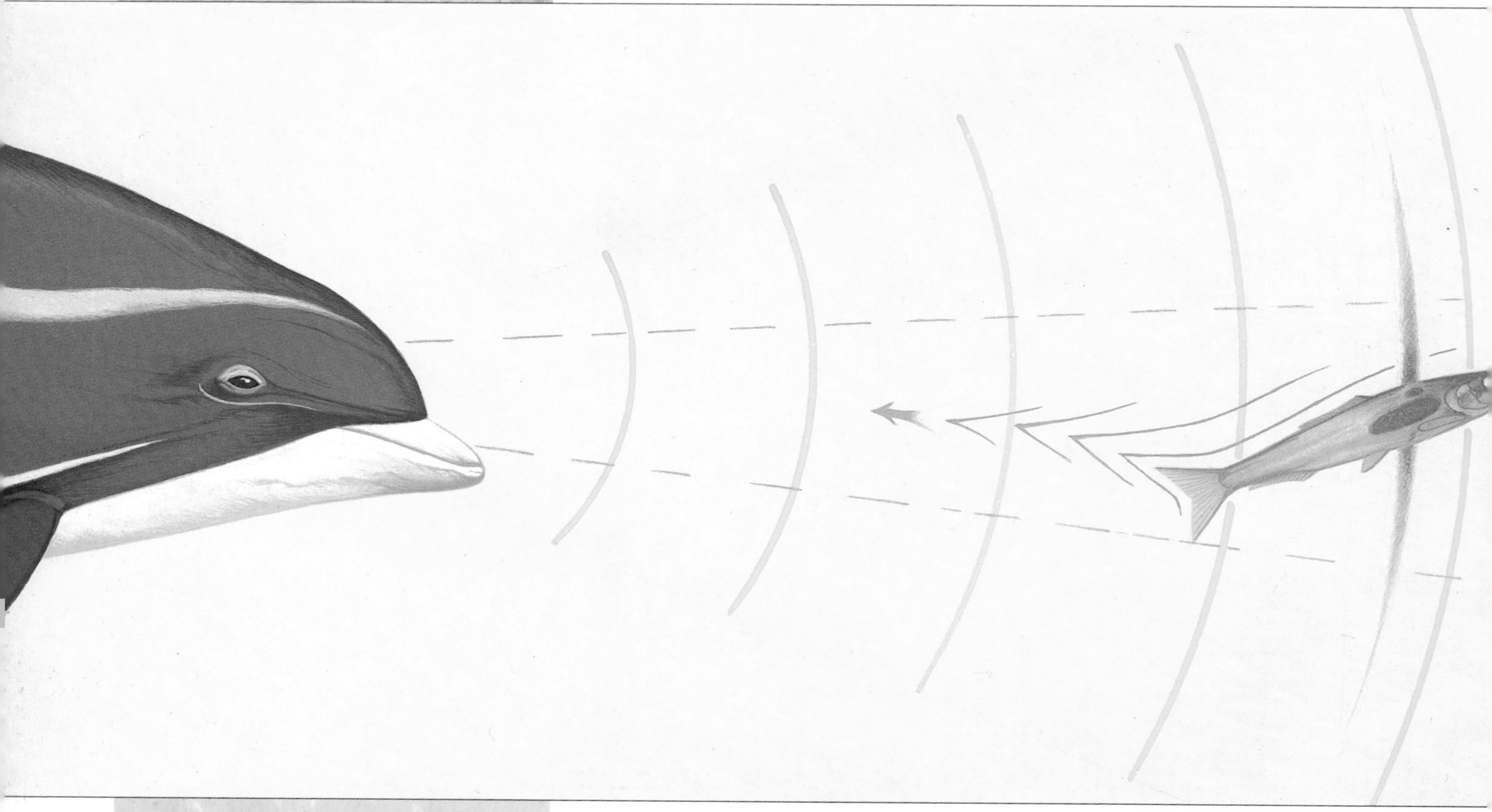

Dolphins are able to build up a 'sound picture' of their surroundings using a remarkable form of sonar, called 'echolocation'. They emit clicking noises that bounce back from other animals, or inanimate objects in the water, and then analyse the echoes.

Echolocation is a sophisticated form of sonar (**SO**und **N**avigation **A**nd **R**anging). It is similar, in theory, to the echo-sounding used by ships to measure water depth and to detect everything from shoals of fish to submarines. The basic principle is simple: pulses of sound are transmitted into the ocean, and any echoes bouncing back are monitored and interpreted. But the system used by dolphins is so complex and sophisticated that it leaves human sonar experts gasping – the human system, although useful, is little more than a crude imitation by comparison.

Echolocation and sonar are frequently confused with radar (**RA**dio **D**etection **A**nd **R**anging). This works on the same basic principle, but uses electromagnetic radiation instead of sound. High-powered pulses, with wavelengths lying somewhere between infrared waves and radio waves, are sent out by a transmitting aerial, reflected back by objects in their path, and then displayed on a computer screen.

Dolphins use echolocation for a variety of purposes – to keep track of one another; to identify changes in sea-floor profile; for navigation; to monitor their surroundings for potential predators or prey; and to hunt. The system has three main advantages over sight. It enables the animals to function efficiently in turbid water, in the dark depths of the ocean, or at night; it has a maximum range of hundreds of metres and therefore, even in daylight, works well beyond the normal visual range; and, since sound waves carry much more information than light, it allows the dolphins to 'see' in three dimensions instead of only two.

It is such an efficient system that, using this acoustic sense alone, a dolphin can discriminate between practically identical objects (even in a noisy environment), and can even investigate two different objects simultaneously (by directing two separate pulses at different angles on either side of the head).

Echolocation clicks Dolphins do not have vocal chords, but produce the sounds required for echolocation internally, probably at structures known as the 'monkey lips', which embrace the upper air passages below the blowhole. Emitted in the form of clicks, these are quite different to the whistles, groans, squeals, barks and other sounds they use to communicate with one another. These clicks are very short in duration – typically less than one millisecond – and may be repeated in rapid succession (although a new click is rarely emitted until the echo of the last one has been received). They are mainly ultrasonic (above the 20 kHz limit of human hearing) but nevertheless range across a broad band from about 0.25 to 220 kHz.

Many people believe that a dolphin's echolocation clicks are focused into a directional beam by a special fatty deposit on the head, known as the 'melon', which can be altered in shape to form a 'sound lens'. The melon appears as a large, bulbous forehead in most species, shown clearly in this bottlenose dolphin.

The clicks are thought to be focused into a directional beam by a special fat deposit, known as the 'melon', on the dolphin's head. Appearing as a large, bulbous forehead in most species, the melon effectively acts as a sound 'lens': it is believed that its shape (and therefore its focal length) can be altered by muscles in the head. (The fat in the melon is unique and, even if the dolphin is malnourished, it is not used as an emergency food source.) The bones of the skull may also assist with focusing, since the forehead seems to form a perfect parabolic reflector.

The nature of the clicking varies according to the dolphin's activity. During normal swimming, for example when looking for food or simply monitoring the environment, a steady, relatively low-frequency clicking is used. If there is something in the water, the time lapse between each click and its echo enables the dolphin to estimate how far away it is; the form of the echo helps to identify its size and shape; and the varying strength, as the echo is received on the two sides of the head, enables the dolphin to evaluate the way in which the object is moving. But when investigating something in more detail, for example when homing in on a fast-moving fish, the dolphin speeds up the clicking (until it is so fast it sounds rather like a creaking door), and focuses it more accurately on the target. This provides much more detailed information on everything from the size of the prey to its texture and even its internal structure.

Studies suggest that dolphins may be able to use echolocation to tell as much about the health and emotional status of other dolphins as we are able to determine from the eyes, facial expressions and body language of other humans.

Echolocation Theories The path taken by the returning echoes to the inner ear is still a subject of debate. Some experts believe that the echoes are received via the small ear holes on either side of the head. But now it seems likely that they are received by the lower jaw and then transmitted through oil-filled sinuses to the inner ear; from there, they travel by nerve impulses to the brain. Since sound travels nearly five times faster in water than in air, and echolocation has become such a highly sophisticated sense, it requires much processing of information. A large part of the dolphin's brain is devoted to making a rapid analysis of the complicated range of echoes constantly being received, in order to form usable images, and then storing this information for future use.

Swimming with dolphins is a strange experience because you *feel* the echolocation clicks as much as *hear* them. They produce an extraordinary tingling sensation, as if your whole body has become one enormous tympanic membrane. Taking this a stage further, it is perhaps not surprising that recent studies suggest that dolphins may be able to use exceptionally powerful blasts of high-frequency sound to stun or even kill their prey. Dolphin researchers jokingly call this the 'big bang' theory. In experimental studies, fish subjected to powerful blasts of sound become disoriented and even immobilized. If dolphins are able to stun fish in this way, it is almost as if they are carrying a loaded gun around with them. It may even explain how they are able to catch fish that could easily out-distance and out-manoeuvre them in a straightforward chase.

There is also a possibility that dolphins can use sonar to 'see' right inside other animals. There is already some evidence that they pay special attention to pregnant women – suggesting that they are able to detect the presence of an unborn child in the mother's womb – and to people with metal plates or pins in their bodies. This sounds rather far-fetched, but it is certainly not impossible. After all, in medicine, where X-rays cannot be used on pregnant women for fear of damaging the foetus, ultrasound scanning is used instead to provide the necessary images. Dolphins use much lower frequencies for their echolocation system, which probably does not give the same fine detail as a medical scan – but instead allows them to 'see' objects from farther away. It is yet another exciting possibility to add to the dolphin's already impressive repertoire of unique sensory skills.

Geomagnetism

The least known of all the dolphin's senses is the ability to detect geomagnetism – in other words, to 'read' the earth's magnetic field. Many animals, from birds and reptiles to bees and bacteria, are believed to have this sixth sense, and there is even some evidence that it exists to a limited degree in humans. It is normally used for navigational purposes, like an invisible map, and may be what we identify in ourselves as simply 'a sense of direction'.

The main evidence for its existence in dolphins lies in recent anatomical studies involving several different species. These have revealed tiny crystals of a magnetic material, a form of iron oxide known as magnetite, in the soft tissues covering the brain. It is believed that these crystals continually orientate themselves in line with natural magnetic force fields, rather like tiny compass needles. By sensing any change in the way they are facing, dolphins may be able to work out the direction in which they themselves are travelling.

There is also strong circumstantial evidence to support this idea. Strandings of live dolphins (mainly open ocean species) have been closely linked to local magnetic, rather than physical, characteristics of the coastline. This suggests that the animals navigate by following magnetic contours (especially where there are no physical features to use as clues) and sometimes make serious mistakes in their 'readings' or are tricked by sudden changes in the contours themselves.

Although direct proof is still lacking, it seems possible that dolphins have developed this unusual sense to a greater degree than most other mammals. But since they may be making serious navigational mistakes on a regular basis, perhaps even they are still experimenting? Geomagnetism is certainly an intriguing area of research, with many new and challenging ideas to investigate.

Many animals, from bacteria to birds, are known to be able to detect the earth's magnetic field. Dolphins may also have this capability, which would enable them to navigate accurately across seas and oceans.

CHAPTER

4

A Day in the Life of a Dolphin

There is really no typical day in the life of a dolphin. It has to cope with so many variables, from weather and sea conditions to food availability and human disturbance, that it must always be taking advantage of certain situations and coping with others. At the same time, daily activities vary from species to species, population to population, and individual to individual, as well as from day to day.

But all dolphins – wherever in the world they live and whatever else is happening around them – have to swim, dive, find food, avoid predators, rest, breed, communicate with other members of their school and do all the other fundamental activities that are essential for survival.

Common dolphins, Sea of Cortez, Mexico.

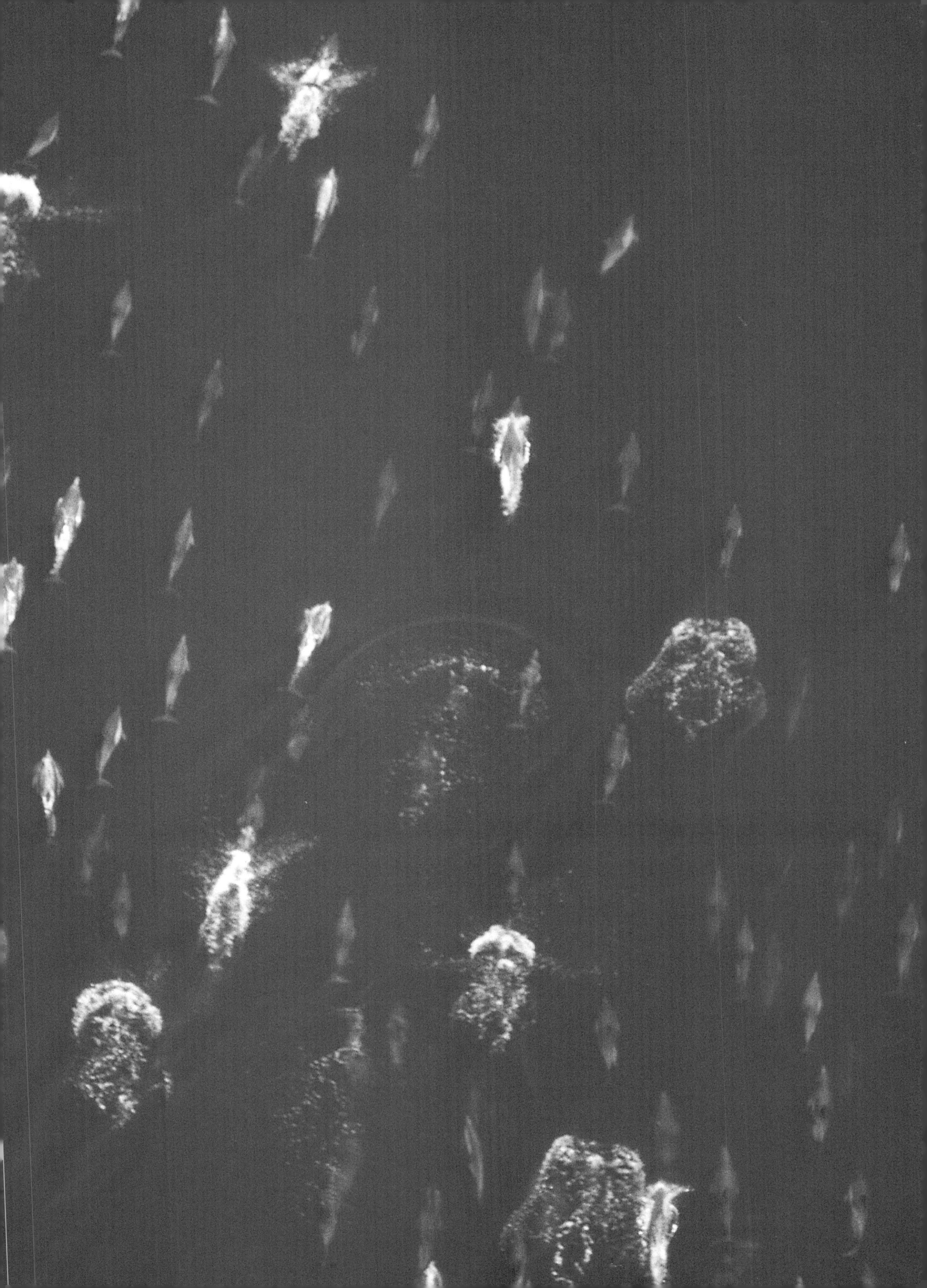

Diving and Swimming

Dolphins are fast and efficient swimmers. They have been clocked at speeds of more than 40 km/h (25 mph), and can swim for long periods without a break. In fact, their swimming performance is so impressive that early calculations and experiments, based on rigid dolphin models, suggested that their achievements were theoretically impossible.

They are not impossible, of course, and the reason that dolphins can outperform laboratory models is because they are able to eliminate frictional drag and turbulence. This is something that no man-made vessel or model has ever achieved. A streamlined body is essential in this respect, but the dolphin's real secret lies in its silky smooth skin. The water closest to the skin creates the most resistance. The skin is designed to minimize this by shedding and renewing the outer cells rapidly (every two hours compared with every eighteen hours in human skin), and by exuding tiny droplets of oil which are believed to act as a lubricant. There is also a system of dermal ridges, similar to the ones that form our fingerprints, found beneath the skin on the back and flanks of most dolphins: these seem to correspond to patterns of water flow. The skin surface is even believed to shift in folds and ripples as a response to changes in pressure on different parts of the body.

The upward movement of the flukes in the water is the power stroke giving propulsion; the downward movement merely returns the flukes to their original position ready for the next stroke.

Dolphins frequently stay underwater for several minutes at a time, and some species can hold their breath for up to a quarter of an hour. This is a remarkable achievement considering that when most people dive underwater, without an artificial air supply, they become acutely distressed after little more than a minute or two; if they are forced to stay under for much longer, there is a serious risk of drowning.

Dolphins breathe in lungfuls of air before they dive. Yet they do not have particularly large lungs, and the air in them plays a very minor role in long, deep dives. This is for two reasons: the amount of oxygen carried in even the largest of lungs would be exhausted very quickly and, since water pressure increases dramatically with depth, any air in the lungs becomes rapidly compressed and reduces to almost nothing long before the dolphins reach their target depth.

Their secret lies in an ability to utilize oxygen extremely efficiently. In fact, even at rest, they need to breathe far less frequently than we do (about four times a minute compared with fifteen times a minute). Firstly, they exchange an incredible 80–90 per cent of their lung volume with each breath (we exchange only 5–15 per cent). Secondly, they extract much more oxygen from the air (as much as 88.5 per cent in some cases). Thirdly, they can store large reserves of oxygen in their blood and muscles (dolphin muscle is very dark

Many dolphins are fast swimmers and some species are able to attain burst speeds of up to 50 kilometres per hour. Their secret lies not only in a streamlined shape and powerful muscles, but also in certain unique characteristics of the skin.

The amount of time spent underwater, and the maximum depth reached, varies greatly from species to species. But oceanic dolphins tend to spend most of their time within 100 metres of the surface.

because of the presence of a protein called myoglobin, which acts as a highly efficient oxygen reservoir). And finally, they can limit the use of oxygen during a dive by slowing down the heart beat (by 50 per cent or more) and restricting blood flow to all but the most vital organs.

Dolphins spend most of their lives within about 100 metres (330 feet) of the surface, but many species are capable of diving much deeper and some can reach depths of at least 500 metres (1,640 feet). Yet they do not seem to suffer from decompression sickness, or 'the bends' as it is more popularly known.

The bends is a potentially fatal condition caused by nitrogen bubbling out of the blood. The deeper human divers go underwater, and the longer they stay there, the more nitrogen is absorbed into their bloodstream from the air in their lungs. At the end of a dive, the pressure increases as they rise to the surface, and the nitrogen begins to come out of solution. This is fine if the divers have not exceeded their dive-time limits; if they return to the surface slowly; and if they make the appropriate decompression stops. But if they do not take these precautions, the nitrogen comes out of solution too quickly, forming small bubbles in the blood vessels and tissues (exactly like the bubbles created in a bottle of fizzy drink when the top is removed and the internal pressure released). These nitrogen bubbles can lodge in joints, causing severe pain, or in vital blood vessels, causing paralysis or even death.

Dolphins do not suffer from the bends, even when they race to the surface from a considerable depth, for several reasons. Since they hold their breath when they dive, they are not continually taking in more air, and so there is relatively little nitrogen to dissolve in the blood and tissues. At the same time, their lungs collapse under pressure and all the remaining air is forced into the thick-walled windpipe and nasal passages, from where no nitrogen can be absorbed into the blood. In most dolphins, the lungs probably collapse completely when they go deeper than about 100 metres (330 feet), mainly because most of the ribs are not joined to the breastbone (and those that do join make contact with long, flexible tendons).

Human divers can suffer from a second potentially dangerous condition, called nitrogen narcosis, which is also more of a problem on deep dives. The

effects are quite similar to those caused by too much alcohol. At a depth of around 30 metres (100 feet) responses are delayed, judgement begins to deteriorate and there is a general feeling of over-confidence; the symptoms intensify as the divers go deeper. Induced by breathing nitrogen under pressure, it does not affect dolphins because they breathe it only at the surface.

Feeding

Dolphins are hunters and spend a considerable amount of their time, day and night, finding and eating food.

Most dolphins feed on fish or squid, but octopuses, crustaceans, molluscs and other invertebrates also feature in the diets of some species. They are opportunistic feeders and tend to eat a mixture of prey species according to their availability at different times of the year. Even those that concentrate on fish, for example, are likely to eat a range of different kinds and they will search for solitary fish hiding on the seabed as well as shoaling fish in the open water.

Unlike large whales, dolphins do not seem to migrate long distances with the seasons, although their constant search for food often requires a fair amount of day-to-day travelling. They often follow their prey or, from experience, know where to intercept it at certain times of the year.

Many dolphins are able to hunt successfully on their own, but if there is enough food to go round there are advantages in pooling resources and hunting in schools. A group of dolphins is likely to be more efficient at finding food than one on its own and, once a shoal has been found, they can help one another to catch the fish. Schools can range in size from a handful of individuals to hundreds or even thousands which all travel, feed and rest together.

A large school normally hunts by splitting into smaller groups and spreading out over a large area of sea, almost like policemen searching for clues around a crime scene. As soon as they have located a shoal of fish, they surround it on all sides and begin to swim in ever-tightening circles. They often corral the shoal against the surface of the water, which acts as an impenetrable barrier (the fish can often be seen jumping frantically into the air in a desperate bid to escape). Limited evidence suggests that the dolphins then take it in turns to dive into the tightly packed shoal to pick off their victims. In some cases, the dolphins may stun the fish with exceptionally powerful echolocation clicks or with their tail flukes, whacking them so hard that they are thrown clear of the water.

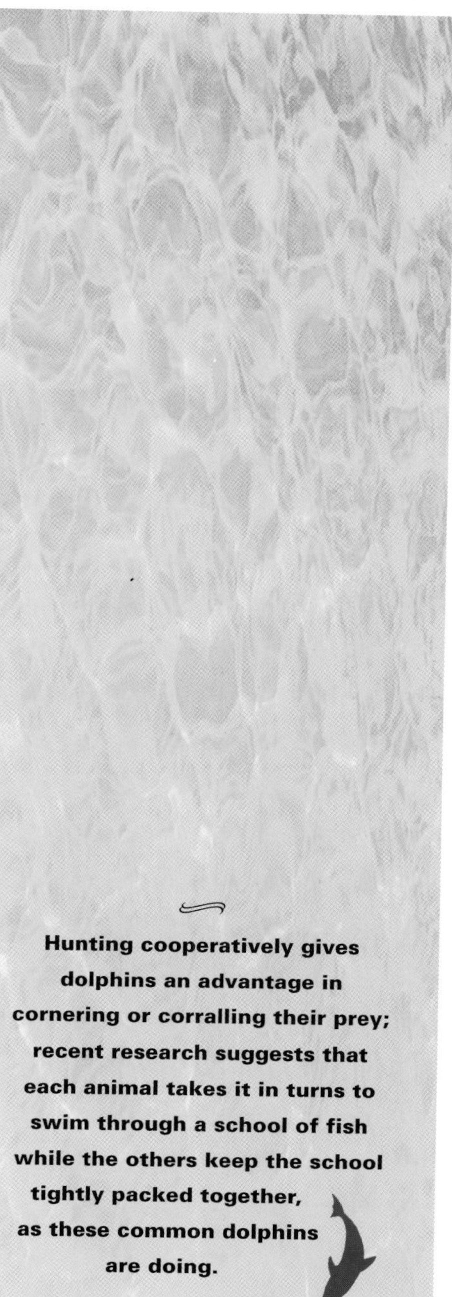

Hunting cooperatively gives dolphins an advantage in cornering or corralling their prey; recent research suggests that each animal takes it in turns to swim through a school of fish while the others keep the school tightly packed together, as these common dolphins are doing.

Playful leaps, breaches and other acrobatics may be the equivalent of 'dinner bells' to other dolphins, signalling the presence of food, or they may help to herd prey animals in a particular direction.

Such cooperative hunting requires a highly refined system of communication, extremely close collaboration or expert leadership, and a high level of trust. It is all the more extraordinary when several species of dolphin hunt side by side (although it is unclear whether they are feeding separately or coordinating their manoeuvres and hunting as one group).

Most cetaceans never touch land at any stage during their lives, unless they are unwell or lost. However, there are a few minor exceptions, especially when it comes to the never-ending search for food. Killer whales, belugas and bottlenose dolphins are known, on occasion, to venture deliberately into such shallow areas that their weight is taken by the beach and not the water itself (although they normally move back into deeper water after a few seconds). Bottlenose dolphins in places as far apart as the Black Sea and South Carolina are known to drive fish onto the land and literally beach themselves amid the floundering prey, which they grab as they slide back into the water.

Dolphins physically catch their food with simple, peg-like teeth. These are designed for grasping slippery, fast-moving animals rather than for chewing and, indeed, dolphins generally swallow their prey whole. They do not have saliva, which in humans helps to break down food ready for digestion in the stomach, because the seawater would wash it away. Instead, their throats and stomachs are able to process large chunks of food.

The stomach contents of dead animals washed ashore or killed by fishermen offer the best clues to a dolphin's diet. It is extremely rare to see a wild dolphin actually catching its prey – let alone to be able to identify the prey species – so biologists have examined the stomach contents of many thousands of dolphins over the years. Studies in captivity can supplement these results with information on the amount of food eaten by different species.

Avoiding Predators

Dolphins have few major predators other than humans. Sharks and certain members of their own family, the Delphinidae, pose the only real threats.

Remains of dolphins have been found in the stomachs of a number of sharks, including tigers, bulls, duskies and great whites. Since these are some of the most powerful and efficient predators on the planet, it would be surprising if dolphins did *not* fall prey to them. In some parts of the world, sharks seem to be quite a serious threat and dolphins tend to move into shallow, inshore waters (which are presumably safer) at times when the sharks are in the vicinity and hunting.

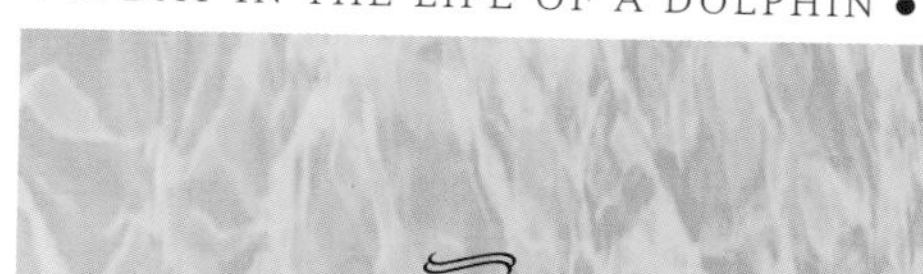

It is often claimed that dolphins are able to kill sharks, by ramming them with their beaks; certainly, a large dolphin would be a powerful adversary for a medium-sized shark such as this Caribbean reef shark.

However, dolphins seem able to judge when they need to take evasive action. They certainly do not panic every time a shark swims nearby and, in fact, the two animals often hunt schools of fish within a stone's throw of each other. Therefore, despite what swimmers and divers have been told for years, it is a myth that if there are dolphins in the water there are no sharks. Obviously, the dolphins are not likely to hang around if there are particularly large or dangerous sharks in the vicinity, but they do not seem especially bothered by most of the others. After all, small or medium-sized sharks would probably treat a fully grown bottlenose dolphin, for example, or some other large dolphin, with considerable respect.

There are many examples of dolphins acting quite calmly in the company of sharks. In fact, there are reports of them harassing sharks – even quite large hammerheads and other potential dolphin-eaters – almost as if they thrive on the risks involved. At the same time, they often seem to be aware that sharks pose a threat to people; stories of dolphins herding them away from swimmers in the water are quite common.

The cetaceans known to hunt dolphins are killer whales (although only certain pods), false killer whales, and to a lesser extent pygmy killer whales and melon-headed whales. Killer whales have been observed hunting dolphins with a technique similar to the one the dolphins use for catching fish: they circle the herd, forcing the prey tighter and tighter, and then take it in turns to rush into the centre and grab a victim. As with sharks, the dolphins do not automatically panic every time they see a killer whale. They seem to be aware that some killer whales are only interested in eating fish, but they steer clear of the pods that feed on marine mammals. Melon-headed whales seem to be more opportunistic, and have been reported attacking dolphins as they escape from the purse-seine nets set for tuna in the Eastern Tropical Pacific (see Chapter 9).

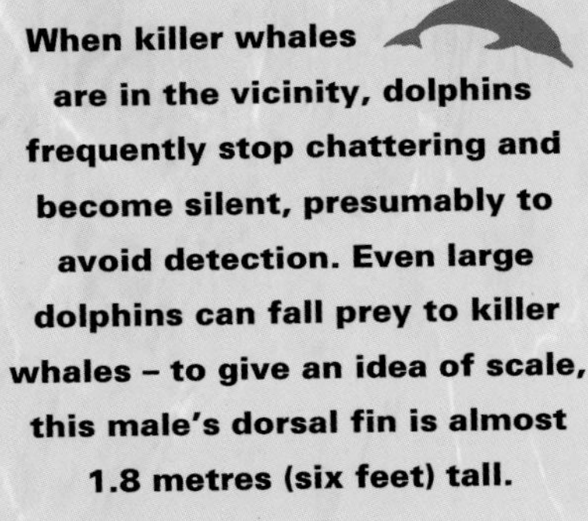

When killer whales are in the vicinity, dolphins frequently stop chattering and become silent, presumably to avoid detection. Even large dolphins can fall prey to killer whales – to give an idea of scale, this male's dorsal fin is almost 1.8 metres (six feet) tall.

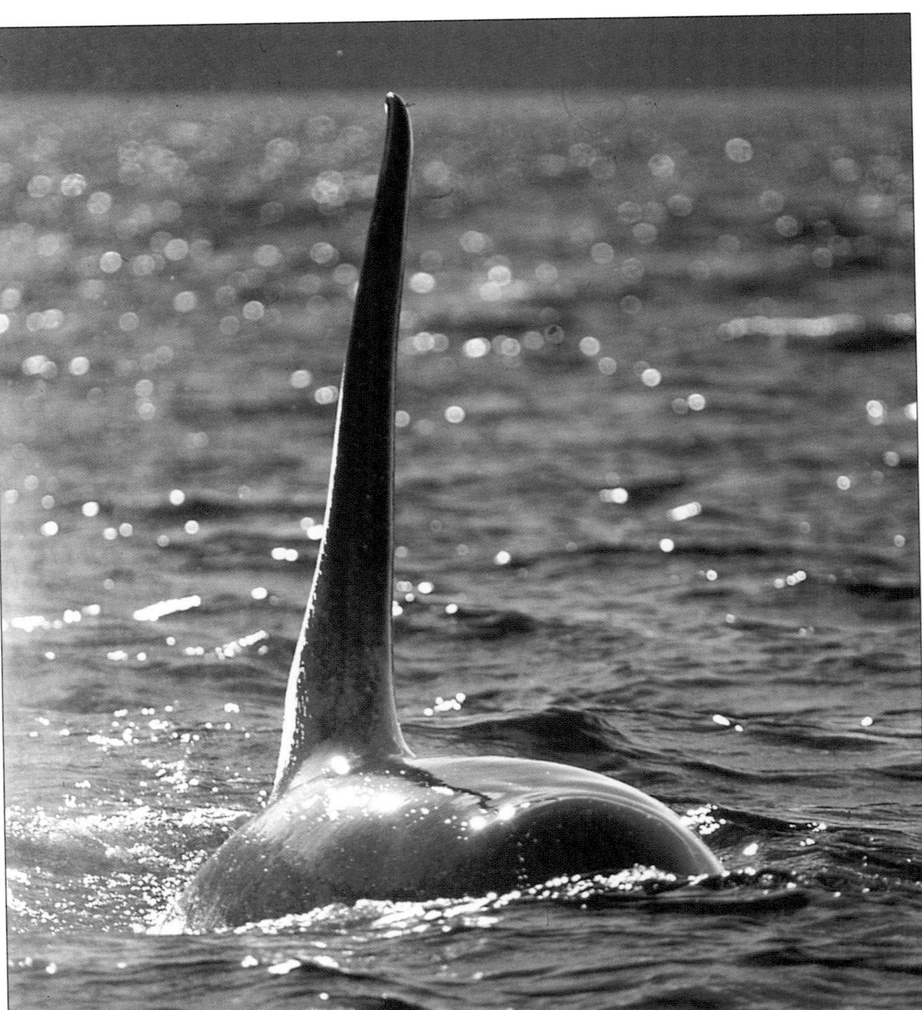

Most dolphins possess a natural camouflage called counter-shading. The upper side of the body is dark and, when seen from above, blends in with the dark depths of the ocean; the lower side of the body is relatively light and, when seen from below, blends in with the light waters at the surface. The bottlenose dolphin, for example, is generally dark grey, charcoal or brown on its back; this gradually pales down the sides until it becomes pale cream or pinkish on the under side. A large school gains extra protection from the visual confusion that a mass of twisting, turning, identical bodies generates, making it much harder for a predator to select a single target and close in for the kill.

Little is known about how much dolphins use self-defence when faced with a predator. There have been reports of them killing sharks by ramming them with their beaks, striking tremendous blows with the full weight of their bodies behind. If they hit in the right place – for example, in the liver – they can probably cause tremendous damage, and may even kill a sizeable attacker. But the common response to a predator attack appears to be for the dolphins to flee: they fall completely silent, form a tight group (if they can) and swim for their lives.

Keeping in Touch

The sea was once thought to be a silent world, whose inhabitants were believed to make little or no noise. But in recent years modern high-tech equipment has enabled us to eavesdrop on life underwater – and it is anything but silent. Invertebrates, fish and marine mammals all make a wide variety of sounds as they go about their daily business and communicate with one another.

Dolphins, in particular, live in a world that is dominated by sound. They cannot rely on sight underwater, because it is often dark (at night or at depth) and in many seas and oceans the visibility can be very poor. Just a few metres is often enough to lose visual contact and, even in the clearest seas, animals more than 100 metres (330 feet) away would be completely out of touch.

However, making noises underwater is not as simple as it may seem. Humans talk by forcing air through vocal chords in the larynx, which vibrate to make sound, but we cannot talk underwater. Scuba divers normally deal with this problem by tapping their air tanks with a metal knife to attract the attention of their co-divers, and then communicating with a system of internationally recognized hand signals.

Dolphins do not have vocal chords. They produce sound internally, probably at structures known as the 'monkey lips', which embrace the upper air passages below the blowhole. They can make a wide variety of sounds, including whistles, clicks, squeaks, squawks, trills, barks and grunts. It is believed that these help to identify individuals and particular groups, to coordinate hunting activities, to convey information such as sexual interest, danger, anger and irritation, and generally to keep in touch. Each dolphin is believed to have its own 'signature whistle', which is almost the equivalent of a human name. It uses this to attract the attention of other dolphins and to identify itself. There is even some evidence to suggest that one dolphin will call the name of another in its group, indicating a sense of self and other.

Dolphins also use body language as a non-vocal form of communication. They slap the water with their bodies, a flipper, their fin or their tail. They blow bubbles, clap their jaws, nod their heads, arch their backs and twist their bodies. Indeed, it is likely that vocal communication and body language are used in tandem, which substantially increases the amount of information that can be conveyed at any one time.

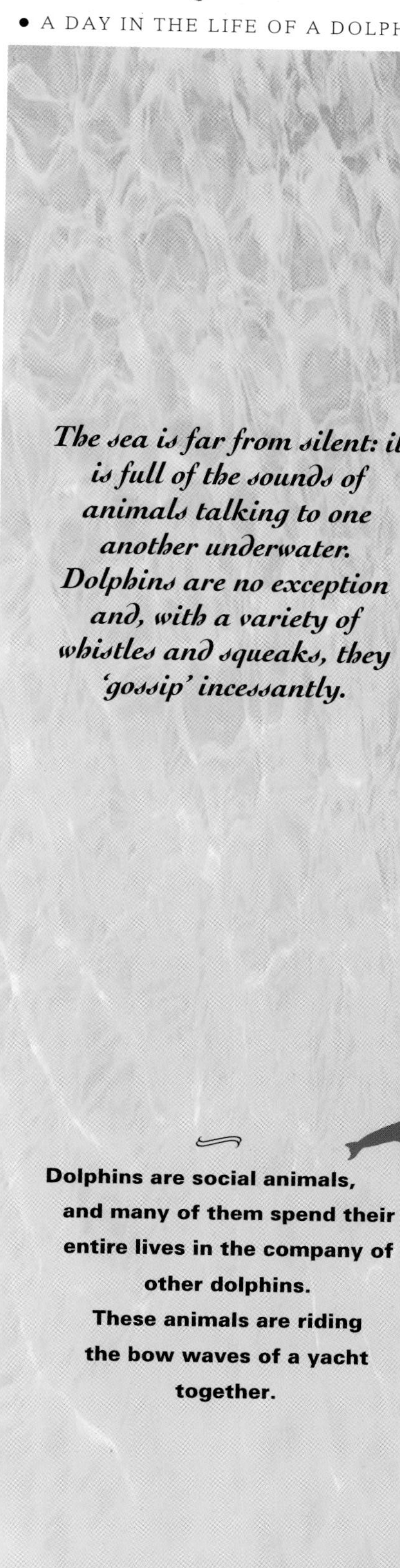

The sea is far from silent: it is full of the sounds of animals talking to one another underwater. Dolphins are no exception and, with a variety of whistles and squeaks, they 'gossip' incessantly.

Dolphins are social animals, and many of them spend their entire lives in the company of other dolphins. These animals are riding the bow waves of a yacht together.

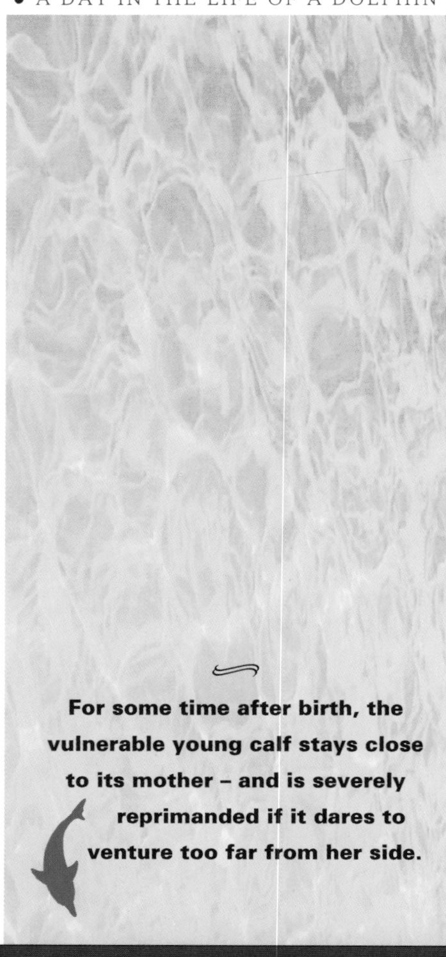

For some time after birth, the vulnerable young calf stays close to its mother – and is severely reprimanded if it dares to venture too far from her side.

Births, Marriages and Deaths

Dolphins are very promiscuous animals. They spend as much as a third of their waking hours in sexual play and do not form long-term pair bonds. Calves as young as six weeks old will copulate with adults (including their own mothers), males regularly couple with other males, females rub genitals with other females, and individuals of either sex may copulate with a range of different partners several times a day. It is not unknown for them to copulate with other species or even different genera, and bottlenose dolphins, in particular, have often shown varying degrees of sexual interest in humans.

It is a puzzle why they 'waste' so much time and energy on all this sexual activity, since they clearly do not mate simply to reproduce. What is its survival value? One suggestion is that dolphins indulge in sex purely for pleasure, like humans. But it is more likely that sex plays a vital role in establishing and reaffirming relationships between members of a group – the equivalent of social grooming in primates.

The more serious business of mating to reproduce is often a long and involved affair. Females rarely conceive more often than once every two or three years, so there is a great deal of competition between males and they will often fight one another for the attention of potential mates. Courting dolphins surface simultaneously, leap out of the water together, play games of chase, touch flippers and caress one another for several hours before mating. The female sends out signals that she is ready to mate (with sound and body language, by changes in the shape and colour of her genital area, or by changes in the chemical composition of her urine and faeces) and the two animals finally

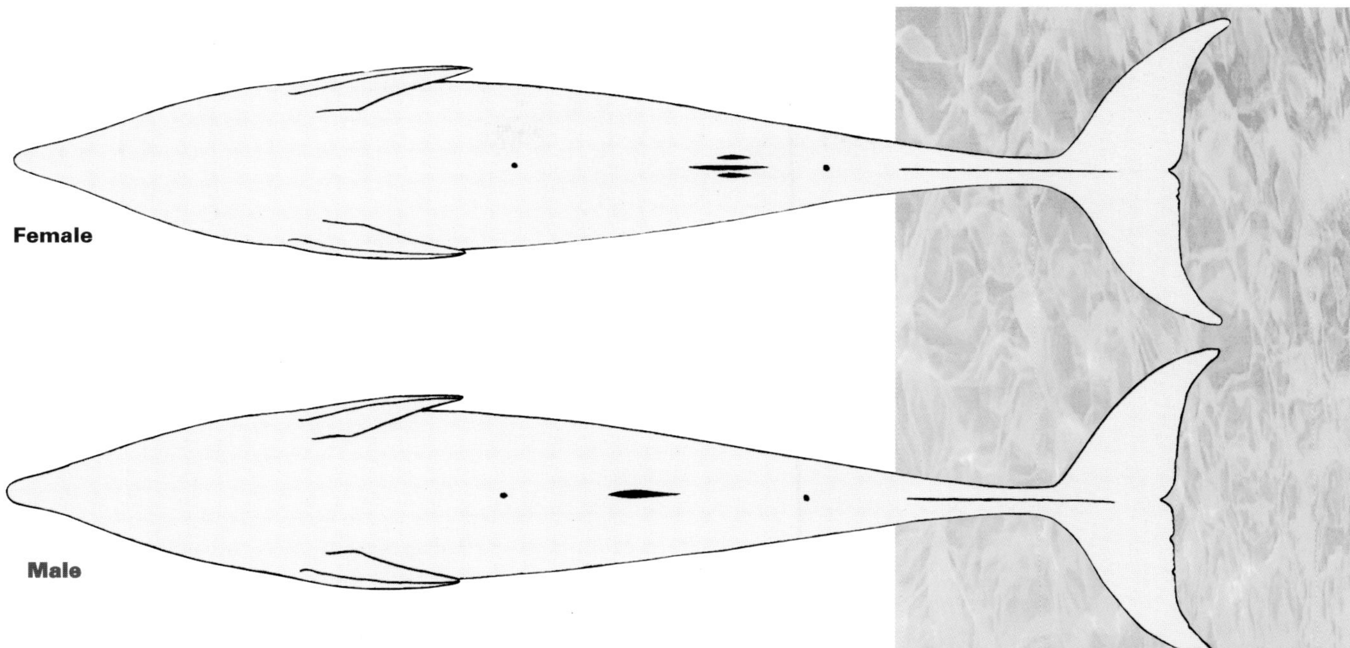

come together, belly to belly. Unlike most large whales, dolphins do not appear to have special mating and calving grounds a long distance from their feeding grounds but, in some species, particularly in higher latitudes, mating does appear to be seasonal.

The gestation period is unknown for many species, but in the majority appears to be ten to twelve months. Like most mammals, dolphins give birth to live young. The single calf is born underwater, near the surface (twins are extremely rare, but not unknown, and normally die soon after delivery). Few births have been witnessed in captivity, and even fewer in the wild, but they appear to be over fairly quickly (normally a matter of twenty or thirty minutes but sometimes several hours). It was once believed that, unlike land mammals which are normally born head-first, dolphin calves appear tail-first; but recent evidence suggests that head-first deliveries are more common than previously thought.

The birth is often assisted by dolphin 'aunts' – other members of the school who act as midwives. They keep sharks and curious males at bay and, if difficulties arise, support the female underneath her body. They have also been known to chew through the umbilical cord, although the female usually breaks it herself with a sudden twist of her body. After the birth, aunts will often guide the new-born dolphin to the surface for its first breath (it knows instinctively

It is extremely difficult to tell the sex of a dolphin without closely examining its underside. As this diagram shows, both males and females have a navel, genital slit and anus; however, in females, the genital slit is much closer to the anus and small mammary slits are usually visible on either side.

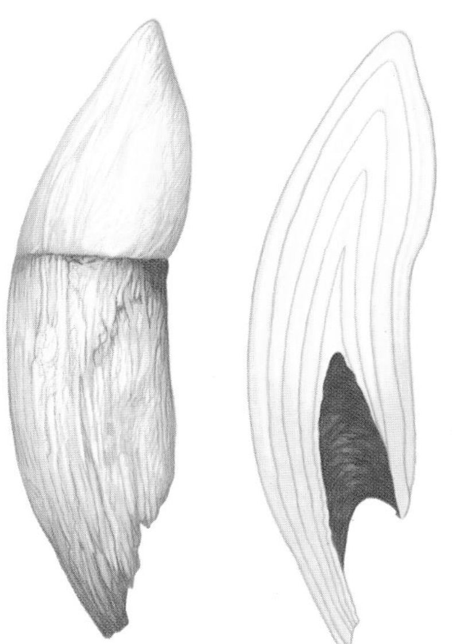

It is possible to estimate the age of dolphins by slicing one of their teeth in half with a very finely cutting guillotine and then, under a microscope, counting the growth layers. These are rather like the growth rings in a tree, although they are much more difficult to count and to interpret.

open its blowhole until it reaches the surface) and they continue to show a great deal of interest for many months afterwards. They even babysit while the mother goes on feeding expeditions. Meanwhile, the father does not appear to be involved in any of these activities and seems to have no active role after mating.

The new-born calf looks like a miniature version of its parents, although there are often subtle differences in shape and body markings. It frequently has marked vertical lines, or 'foetal folds', on its flanks for a few hours after birth (probably a result of being crumpled inside its mother's womb) but these soon disappear. It may also have bristles around the beak, a left-over from the dolphin's prehistoric terrestrial beginnings.

The baby dolphin is born with open eyes and enough muscular coordination to swim with its mother immediately after birth. It swims a little awkwardly at first and, for some time, seems to be attached to its mother's side by an invisible thread. The two animals often touch one another and rise simultaneously to take breaths of air, although it takes a few months for the youngster to perfect the graceful surfacing of its mother. This extreme closeness provides a form of camouflage, helping the two animals to blend together and thus making the new-born calf less obvious to predators, and it may also help the calf to save energy by hitching a ride in the slipstream created as its mother moves through the water.

The calf is suckled underwater (near the surface so that both mother and baby can come up for air) and the milk is squirted directly into a tube formed by its tongue against the roof of the mouth. Dolphin milk is extremely rich and contains considerably more fat and less water than the milk of most land mammals. It consists of 20–40 per cent fat, 10–16 per cent protein and no lactose (compared with only 2–3 per cent fat, 1 per cent protein and 6.5 per cent lactose in humans). Suckling continues for more than a year in most species, although some start to eat solid food within a few months of birth.

Dolphins suffer from many diseases and other health problems that also afflict humans, including cancers, stomach ulcers, heart disease and pneumonia.

The young dolphin remains under its mother's care and tutelage for several years. This is when it learns and practices many of the skills essential for survival in adulthood, from communicating with other members of the school and avoiding predators to finding and catching food. Gradually, the youngster becomes more adventurous. But the maternal bond is continually re-affirmed by constant physical contact and, if it strays too far from its mother's side, she will rush over and chastise it severely (by slapping with her flukes or biting). As the calf grows older, the maternal bond begins to weaken and it spends more and more time with other young dolphins, eventually leaving altogether to join a group of subadults.

It is unknown how long most dolphins live. Many are killed by predators or people, or in accidents caused by anything from collisions with boats to swallowing stingray barbs. They also suffer from a long list of diseases, including cancers, stomach ulcers, pneumonia, heart disease, jaundice and a variety of others familiar to humans; and they are afflicted by a great many internal parasites, including nematodes, hook worms, lung mites and tapeworms, that can cause severe weakness or death. They may even be killed, on occasion, by prey fighting back: one bottlenose dolphin in Portugal was seen frantically trying to dislodge an octopus that had covered its blowhole.

The maximum life span may be as high as fifty years in some species, although it is probably much lower in many others. Bottlenose dolphins are believed to have a maximum life span in the wild of at least twenty-five years in males and thirty years in females, although even these figures are likely to vary from one region to another.

The Social Life of a Dolphin

Dolphins are social animals, and many of them spend their entire lives in the company of other dolphins. But there is more to living together than simply an innate 'friendliness', and dolphin schools vary in size and composition according to requirements. It is a survival strategy. Living together improves the chances of finding and catching food; increases the likelihood of spotting and avoiding predators; makes it easier to encounter a suitable mate; provides a resource of willing and available babysitters to help look after calves; and increases the learning potential of youngsters.

School sizes vary enormously, from just two animals to tens of thousands spread across vast areas of ocean. Some species are far more sociable than others and certain activities benefit from high numbers more than others. Oceanic dolphins tend to form the largest schools, and these may include several species travelling together. Many years ago, schools of tens of thousands were not uncommon (there are records of some exceeding 100,000), but these days a few thousand is exceptional and a few dozen or a few hundred most common. Inshore dolphins tend to form smaller schools.

The composition of a school varies from species to species, region to region, and day to day (sometimes even from hour to hour). Some schools are stable over periods of months or years, with the same animals spending most of their time together, but most are fairly fluid. The basic unit is the mother and calf,

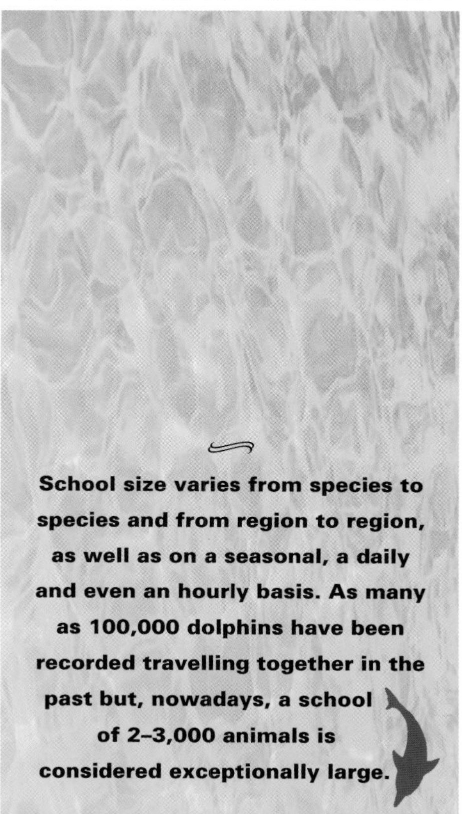

School size varies from species to species and from region to region, as well as on a seasonal, a daily and even an hourly basis. As many as 100,000 dolphins have been recorded travelling together in the past but, nowadays, a school of 2–3,000 animals is considered exceptionally large.

which stay together for many years, but other dolphins come and go quite freely. A 'pecking order' or dominance hierarchy has been observed in dolphins in captivity; limited evidence suggests that this also occurs in the wild. In general, it seems that the larger individuals are the most dominant, but the leadership changes frequently.

Large schools normally contain a mixture of ages and both sexes (although these may be segregated within the herd), but smaller ones are often more exclusive. There are nursery groups, consisting of a number of adult females and their calves; bachelor groups, consisting of adult and young males; and nuclear groups, consisting of adults of both sexes. Travelling together requires

Limited evidence suggests that there is a 'pecking order', or 'dominance hierarchy', in most dolphin schools. Dominance is shown by chasing, biting, ramming, tail slapping and, as in this picture, jaw clapping.

careful coordination, and larger schools tend to travel in formation. If the dolphins are moving from one place to another, for example, they may form a wedge shape, with the dominant animals and those with good navigational skills at the front, and the youngsters protected in the centre.

Within this basic framework, the precise details of their social lives are only just beginning to emerge. Dolphin societies are complex and difficult to study in the wild – and almost impossible to study in captivity. However, modern research techniques, such as photo-identification and DNA fingerprinting, are beginning to shed light on the relationships within a dolphin school, while close-range underwater studies are unravelling some of the secrets of their social behaviour.

How Do Dolphins Sleep?

There are many age-old myths about the way dolphins sleep. Some claim they spend the night curled up on shore, in the company of seals and sealions; others say they simply lie down on the seabed. But the truth is that, unlike most other mammals, dolphins do not have regular sleeping and waking patterns linked to night and day. They do sleep, but not in the way that we do.

The reason is simple. Dolphins cannot fall into a deep sleep (a naturally occurring state of unconsciousness) because their breathing is under conscious control. In other words, they must be awake and able to think in order to breathe. If they were to lapse into a deep sleep, they would drown.

Whenever a dolphin needs to rest, it therefore takes a short cat-nap instead, either suspended just below the surface or while swimming along slowly. To do this, it switches off one half of its brain at a time. While one side is asleep, the other remains awake (to control breathing) and vigilant (to look out for predators). Then the two sides swap. In this semi-conscious state, one eye may be open and the other closed, and the dolphin normally stops vocalizing. For this reason, resting dolphins in a school tend to swim in tight formation, close enough to be able to see each other; if they are disturbed, they stir and chatter for a few moments, but then silence sets in again. It is unlikely that they dream – studies of their brain-wave patterns do not reveal REM (rapid-eye movement), which is normally a sign of dreaming.

Dolphins do not seem to need much sleep. This may be at least partly because water is so much more buoyant than air. With the force of gravity,

Dolphins do not have a regular sleeping and waking pattern linked to night and day and, unlike us, they never fall into a deep sleep. Instead, they take short 'cat-naps', resting only half the brain at a time.

most land-based mammals have to use their muscles simply to stand up and remain balanced, whereas dolphins are able to float and rest their muscles even when they are not actually 'asleep'. On the other hand, it is likely that their sonar system may require rest and repair: after all, it has to produce and interpret untold numbers of echolocation clicks for long periods without a break.

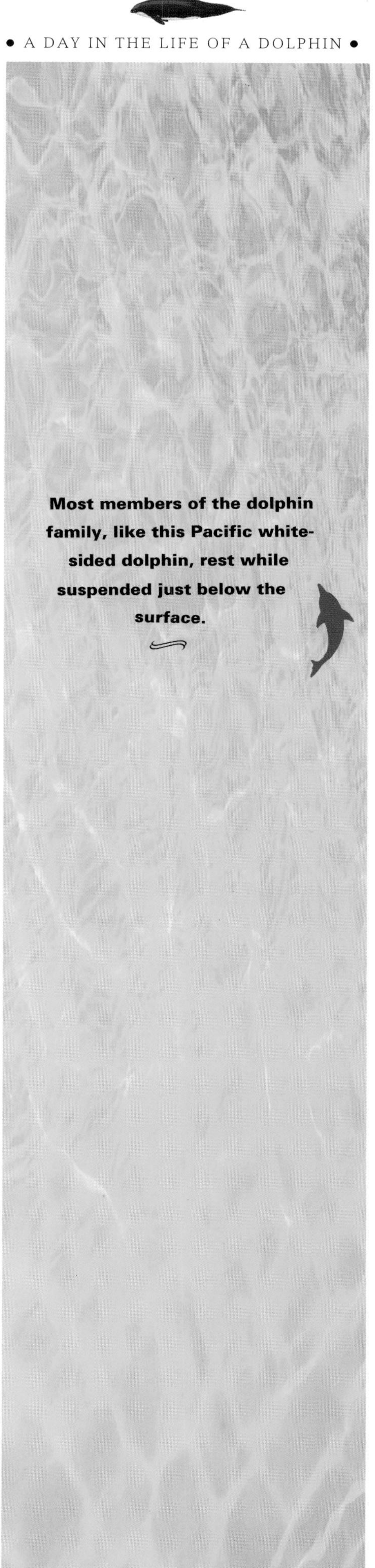

Most members of the dolphin family, like this Pacific white-sided dolphin, rest while suspended just below the surface.

CHAPTER

5

Dolphin Research

More than 2,300 years ago, the basic biology of dolphins was known surprisingly well: the Greek scientist and philosopher Aristotle (384–322 BC) recorded, among other observations, that dolphins are warm-blooded, breathe air and suckle their young. After such an early start, it would be easy to assume that we have learnt almost everything there is to know about dolphins and their lives. Unfortunately, this is far from the case. Research on dolphins in the wild is still in its infancy, and although we know a great deal about a handful of species, we know surprisingly little about all the others.

Fraser's dolphins, St Vincent.

Dolphins are difficult animals to study in the wild and, despite years of research, we are only just beginning to understand a little of their secret lives.

With its relatively long history in captivity, and its predominantly inshore habitat in the wild, the bottlenose dolphin is one of the best known of all cetaceans. Nevertheless, it is still not an easy animal to study.

Sources of Information

The dolphin family includes some of the least-understood large mammals in the world. As one biologist commented at a recent conference, after decades of research our knowledge of them has progressed from almost nothing to just a little bit. Most of what we know about their biology – and virtually everything we know about their lives wild and free – has been learned since the Second World War. But in recent years many more people have become involved in dolphin research, which has developed into a highly sophisticated branch of natural science.

For many years, the only information we had came from dead animals washed ashore or killed by fishermen, and later from captive animals kept in concrete tanks. We had a wealth of data on basic dolphin biology, but our knowledge of their lives under natural conditions was severely limited. Then, in the late 1960s and early 1970s, biologists began to spend more and more time at sea studying wild dolphins. Increasing numbers of people became actively involved in dolphin research (from a few dozen about forty years ago to many hundreds today) and most species are now being studied somewhere in the world.

With a continual flow of new information, our understanding of dolphin biology, behaviour and natural history is changing all the time. In fact, we are only just beginning to understand the intricacies of their behaviour at sea, their diving capabilities, their echolocation system, their ability to detect the earth's magnetic field, and many other aspects of their daily lives.

Studying dolphins is all about being content with tiny snippets of information that have to be assembled into a coherent picture over a period of many years. It is like piecing together an enormously complicated jigsaw puzzle, where every piece brings with it new surprises. The main difference, of course, is that the dolphin puzzle will probably never be completely finished.

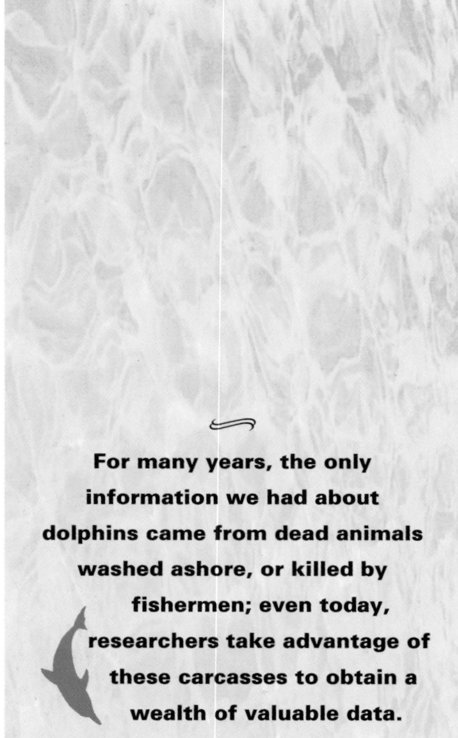

For many years, the only information we had about dolphins came from dead animals washed ashore, or killed by fishermen; even today, researchers take advantage of these carcasses to obtain a wealth of valuable data.

Studying Dead Dolphins

Few scientists these days would contemplate killing a dolphin for research purposes. But there is no denying the wealth of information that can be derived from dead animals which have died naturally, or have been killed accidentally in fishing nets or intentionally for other reasons.

A comprehensive study of a dead dolphin is always time-consuming, and can often be incredibly smelly and rather unpleasant. Typically, the study breaks down into three distinct stages, which may or may not be carried out by the same person.

The first stage is a basic post-mortem, which takes place on site (if the animal cannot be transported) or in a laboratory. It involves taking external and internal body measurements (everything from total length to the thickness of the blubber); identifying the sex and checking the reproductive status (for example, if it is a female, whether it is lactating or pregnant); and making detailed notes on the general health of the animal, paying particular attention to any serious injuries and obvious signs of disease or parasites (this may also identify the cause of death, if it is not already known).

The second stage is the analysis of all the samples obtained during the post-mortem, and this nearly always takes place in a laboratory. An astonishing amount of information can be gleaned from a single carcass and, when this is combined with similar information from other carcasses, it becomes invaluable.

The teeth are sectioned and prepared for examination under a microscope; by counting the growth layers (rather like counting the annual rings in a tree) it is possible to estimate the age of the dolphin. By combining this figure with the measurements of its length and weight, it is possible to estimate how fast the animal grew. Tissue samples from the blubber, muscle, liver and other parts of the body are chemically analysed, providing information on the build-up of organochlorines, heavy metals and other pollutants in the body tissue. A sample of the skin is taken to work out the genetic make-up; by obtaining a 'DNA fingerprint', it is possible to investigate the dead animal's relationships with other animals found in the same region. And the stomach contents are examined to identify the type and size of prey taken during the last meal, thus providing valuable information on the dolphin's diet.

The sexual organs are also studied, and these can reveal a wealth of further information. For example, in a female, the ovaries contain a permanent life record of the number of ovulations she has had and, indirectly, how many calves she has produced. The mammary glands and uterus also provide information on the reproductive state of the animal at the time of its death. In a male, it is possible to make similar deductions by microscopic examination of tissue from the testes. With this kind of information and, of course, a sufficiently large sample of dead animals, it is possible to estimate the average age of sexual maturity; the length of time between calves; the typical gestation period; the length of time the mothers produce milk; peak months for breeding; the overall reproductive rate of the population; and much more.

The precise nature of the laboratory work depends largely on the aims of the project, and the information required. In some cases, the biologist may be

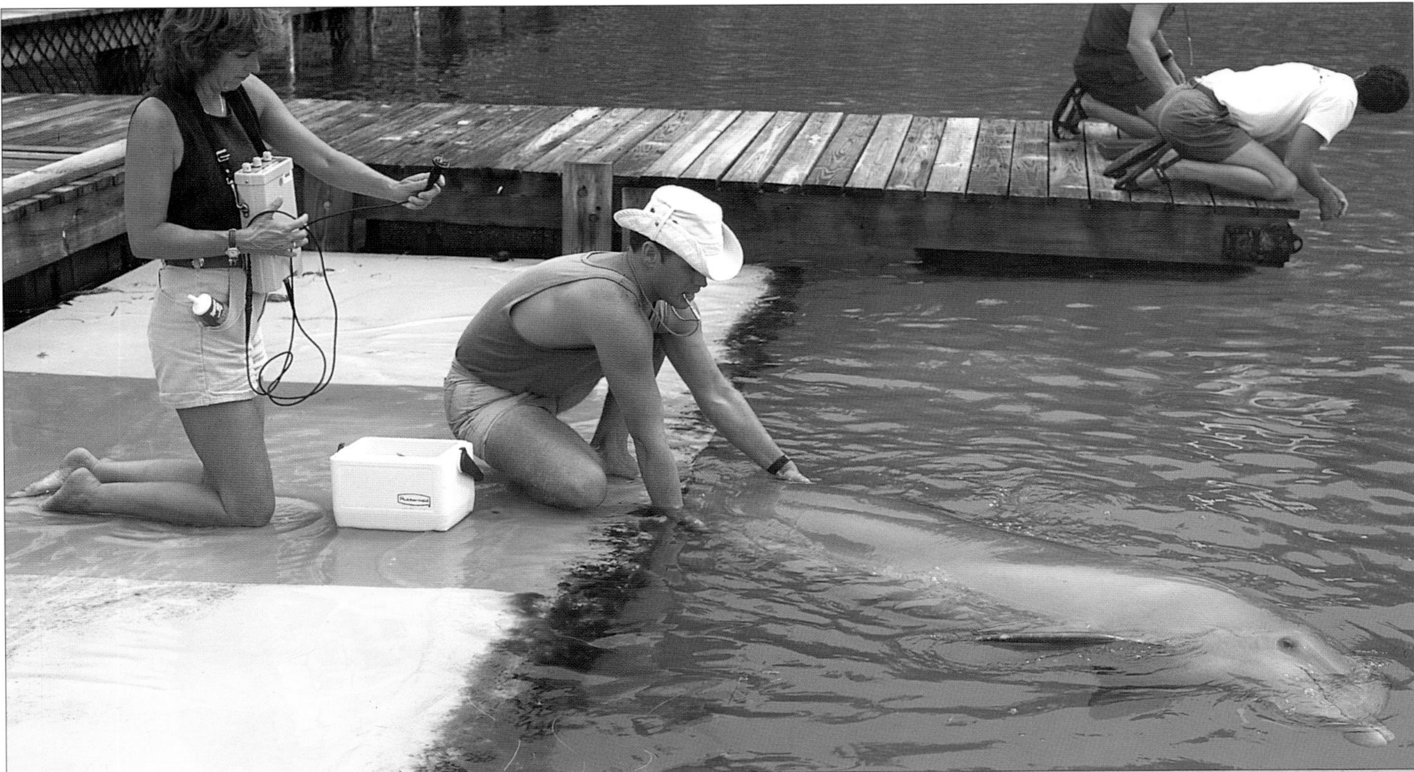

concerned only with the melon, skull or spinal column, for example, and time and financial constraints may make a more general post-mortem impossible.

The third and final stage in the study is the subsequent analysis of all the results. This normally takes place in front of a computer screen in an office, and is often the most time-consuming stage of all. What do the results mean? How do they compare with findings in other parts of the world? Are they statistically significant? What further research needs to be done? These and many other questions need to be answered before the work can finally be written up and published.

Field Observation

There are many aspects of a dolphin's life which can be learnt only by patient observation. In the early days of dolphin research, most live studies were carried out with captive bottlenose dolphins, which have always seemed to cope with the constraints of captivity better than most other species. However, in the last two decades, increasing numbers of people have taken to the sea, in order to take up the challenge of studying dolphins living wild and free in their natural environment.

Researching dolphins in the wild is both challenging and expensive, because the animals are so difficult to study. Many species live in remote areas far out to sea, spend much of their lives underwater and often show little of themselves when they rise to the surface to breathe. Some are also shy and elusive (and frequently avoid boats), which makes close encounters with them almost impossible.

Early research efforts in the late 1960s and early 1970s concentrated mainly on counting dolphins at sea. Observers were posted on land, in boats or in light aircraft, and used relatively simple methods to calculate school and population sizes. There is still no perfect way to count dolphins, but the techniques are being refined all the time and, nowadays, surveys take into account everything from the number of animals likely to have been missed along a cruise track to varying sea and weather conditions.

Studying dolphins in captivity has offered a chance to do research that would otherwise have been extremely difficult, or even impossible, to do in the wild. Unfortunately, in addition to the moral dilemma about captive dolphins, the results may not always be representative of dolphins living wild and free. Further research is often needed, under natural conditions, before firm conclusions can be drawn.

Since dolphins spend the majority of their lives underwater, it is important for researchers to enter their world as well as observing them at the surface.

Wild dolphin research is still in its infancy but, as more high-tech equipment becomes available and more researchers get into the field, it is becoming quite a sophisticated branch of natural science.

In recent years, there have been some ingenious developments which take the studies well beyond sheer numbers. During the course of their work, many dolphin researchers enlist the help of satellites in space, radio transmitters, high-tech directional hydrophones, complex computer programmes, fibre optics, and even the latest DNA fingerprinting techniques. They still spend time simply watching dolphins through binoculars, or doing things like leaning out of boats to scoop up faeces, but now they have all this state-of-the-art equipment at their disposal as well.

Since a remarkable project in Kealakekua Bay, Hawaii, in the 1960s, when spinner dolphins were the subject of the first extended underwater study of wild dolphins, a number of researchers have made a special effort to penetrate the dolphin's underwater world. Some don wetsuits and scuba or snorkelling equipment, then dive in to swim amongst them on a one-to-one basis; others prefer to use research submersibles.

Kenneth Norris, world-renowned for his outstanding work on whales and dolphins over many years, developed a particularly interesting purpose-built dolphin watching boat for underwater observation. He called it the Mobile Observation Chamber (MOC) or, more popularly, the Semi-Submersible Seasick Machine (SSSM). Unfortunately, it was so slow – and so frightening for observers locked in the underwater viewing chamber in anything but calm seas – that its operations had to be restricted to sheltered bays. Despite its flaws, the SSSM encouraged other people to develop larger and much grander research submersibles; gradually, they are delving deeper and deeper into the dolphin's world.

Photo-identification

In many wildlife research projects, it is important to be able to identify individual animals in order to follow their daily activities. In the past, this was frequently done by capturing them and then marking them with large, brightly-coloured artificial tags or painted numbers. However, this caused a considerable amount of stress, and sometimes injured the animals as well. These days, many people consider this kind of tagging to be too invasive, and it is more common to use natural markings for identification purposes instead.

Jane Goodall was one of the first people to use natural markings for wildlife research. In her classic study in Gombe National Park, Tanzania, she used facial patterns to recognise all the local chimpanzees; she found that each member of the group had a distinctive haircut, as well as a recognizable mouth and nose, and unique eyes and ears. More recent studies have used striping patterns in zebras, the arrangement of whiskers in lions and even the shapes, nicks, scars and vein patterns on elephants' ears to tell one animal from another.

Ironically, the potential for individual recognition in dolphins was first acknowledged more than 2,300 years ago. Aristotle recorded that fishermen in the eastern Mediterranean could tell one animal from another by the nicks in their dorsal fins. Generations of people dismissed this as fable until the 1970s,

when biologists began to consider the possibility of using natural markings in dolphin research. Their efforts were the beginning of one of the most important developments ever in the study of wild dolphins.

Individual dolphins are normally identified by variations in the shape and size of their dorsal fins and by unique body markings such as scarring or unusual pigmentation patterns. Some of these natural markings may have a genetic basis, but many are caused by parasites, predators and fights with other dolphins; 'man-made' injuries, caused by anything from entanglement in fishing nets to close encounters with boats, can also be used for identification purposes. Some species (and even some populations) have more scratches and scars than others, and are therefore easier to recognise as individuals, so the precise technique used varies accordingly. The dorsal fin is normally the key

Photo-identification has revolutionized the study of wild dolphins, enabling researchers to identify and follow the daily activities of individual animals.

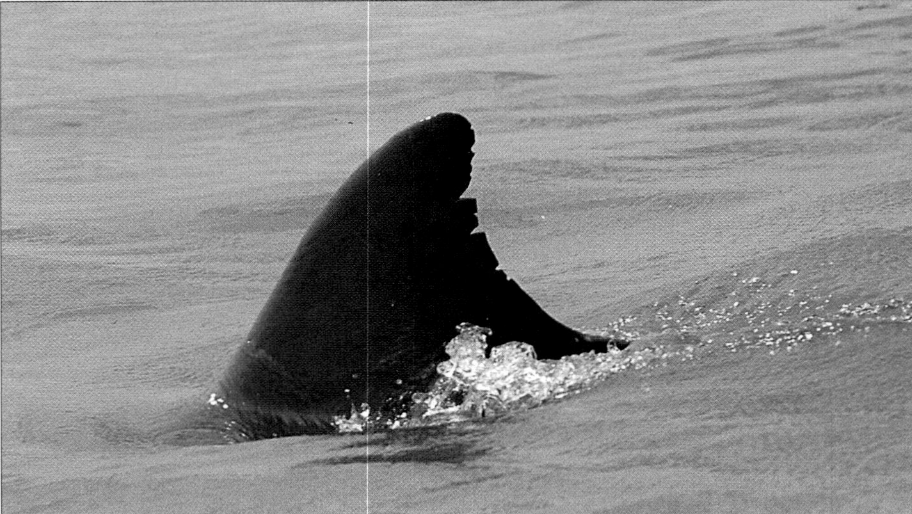

With skill and experience, it is possible to identify individual dolphins by slight variations in the shapes of their dorsal fins, or by unique natural markings such as scarring and pigmentation patterns.

feature in bottlenose dolphins, for example, while body scarring in conjunction with the dorsal fin is important in Risso's dolphins.

With skill and experience, it is sometimes possible to recognise individual dolphins by eye. But few researchers rely entirely on eyesight and memory for their work. The differences between individuals can often be quite subtle and therefore, particularly if a large population is being studied, the risk of human error is high. It is also important to be able to discuss individual dolphins with other researchers, especially when comparing notes on individuals that have been recorded elsewhere.

The solution is to take detailed photographs of each animal – like a series of 'mug-shots' – to confirm their identity and to provide a permanent record of their existence. This technique is known as photo-identification, or simply photo-ID, and it has dramatically extended our knowledge of wild dolphins in recent years.

Unfortunately, as anyone who has tried to photograph dolphins in the wild will know, obtaining good, clear pictures can be extremely difficult. Dolphins are relatively small and fast animals; they rarely spend more than a fraction of a second rising to the surface to breathe, and even then show little of themselves. Add to this the problems of selecting, and then photographing, a single animal in a bustling group... clearly, photo-ID requires a great deal of

Researchers in many parts of the world are compiling 'ID-catalogues' of all the dolphins in their study populations; this particular catalogue is for a population of bottlenose dolphins living near Guayaquil, in Ecuador.

experience, patience and care. It is also a never-ending process. Each animal has to be photographed several times to make a positive identification and, since many natural markings inevitably change over time, it also has to be *re*-photographed at regular intervals during the life of the project. Computers are often used to make the final sorting process faster and more efficient, particularly for checking to see if newly photographed individuals match any of those already on file, but even this can be extremely time-consuming.

Not surprisingly, photo-ID studies can take many years, even decades, to produce meaningful results. Researchers have to build up an intimate knowledge of 'their' animals – and then compare their findings with those of similar studies in other parts of the world. It is a tribute to their perseverance that photographic catalogues containing hundreds of mug-shots have already been prepared for a number of dolphin populations, and it is encouraging that new ones are being started all the time.

By allowing repeated observations of the same dolphins, photo-ID studies are invaluable in a number of ways. They enable researchers to follow their movements and map out their home ranges, to study associations between different individuals, to identify the sequence and timing of key events in their lives, to calculate average life spans, and to recognize differences in behaviour according to their age and sex. They can also be used to study the idiosyncrasies of individual dolphins and to investigate group stability. By following the lives of individual females for many years, it is possible to discover how often they give birth, and whether or not this changes as they grow older, or differs from one population to another. Regular observations of calves can reveal how long they remain with their mothers and, eventually, at what age they themselves start to breed. It is even possible to calculate population sizes, by using the percentage of re-sighted animals to estimate the total number of individuals.

Photo-identification of dolphins is widely acclaimed as one of the most exciting wildlife 'tagging' studies of all time. It has opened up a whole new world of dolphin research, and is already generating a great deal of information that would otherwise have been very difficult – or even impossible – to obtain.

The common dolphin has long been one of the more familiar members of the dolphin family, yet recent research has revealed that it is actually two different species. These have many physical, behavioural and genetic differences, and have been named the short-beaked and long-beaked common dolphins respectively.

Radio and Satellite Telemetry

Telemetry is the use of a radio transmitter, attached in some way to an animal, which sends pulsed signals to remote receivers on land, in boats, in aircraft, or on satellites orbiting the earth. It is invaluable for research purposes, gathering information that was previously unobtainable or that would have required someone to follow the animal within visual range for hours, days or even weeks at a time. However, it is a rather controversial form of research, believed by some to cause unnecessary stress and discomfort to the individual animals being caught, tagged and tracked.

Radio transmitters were first attached to free-living cetaceans in the 1960s. Designed to send signals over relatively short distances, they were so large and so heavy that they could only be used on the larger whales. With the considerable advances in micro-electronics of recent years, however, the transmitters have become much smaller, and are now being used on dolphins and other small cetaceans as well. In years to come, further reductions in size may ultimately enable biologists to fire the transmitters into the blubber from boats, without having to capture the animals first (as they are already doing with large whales).

Radio transmitters have become more sophisticated in recent years as well. Originally, they were used simply as tracking devices: by triangulating the signals sent to different receiving stations, it was possible to locate the animal's

A satellite transmitter sends signals up to a satellite orbiting the earth, which then beams them back down to a powerful receiving station on the ground; from there, the information is sent directly to the researcher along a telephone line.

Kevin Maddison

position at regular intervals and thus follow its movements. They are still used for this purpose, but nowadays the signals may also give details of the animal's physiology and behaviour (everything from swimming patterns to heart rate) and environmental conditions such as water temperature and pressure.

Radio telemetry does have its limitations, however, and can be expensive if boats or aircraft are needed to follow the animals being studied (albeit at a distance). Satellite-linked telemetry is a good alternative. This works on the same basic principle, but the signals are transmitted via satellites rather than directly to receiving stations on earth. The satellites beam the information down to land stations and, from there, it is sent to the researcher's computer along a telephone line. Since satellites continually scan the entire surface of the earth, the study animals can be tracked anywhere and simply cannot 'escape'. There is also no need to spend time and money tracking them by boat or aircraft. Satellite transmitters are expensive to purchase, but their day-to-day operating costs can be lower than traditional radio telemetry.

Apart from the fact that it is an invasive technique, there is one major problem with all forms of telemetry which has yet to be resolved. After a time, the transmitters are rejected by the body tissues of the study animals, and fall into the sea – usually long before their useful lives are over. The challenge now is to develop a way of fixing transmitters to the slippery, wet skin of whales and dolphins in such a way that they remain in position for months or even years at a time – without causing the animals harm.

Radio- and satellite-transmitters, such as the one attached to this Heaviside's dolphin, enable researchers to follow the movements of animals over considerable distances and for long periods of time. However, there is some concern about the invasive nature of this type of research.

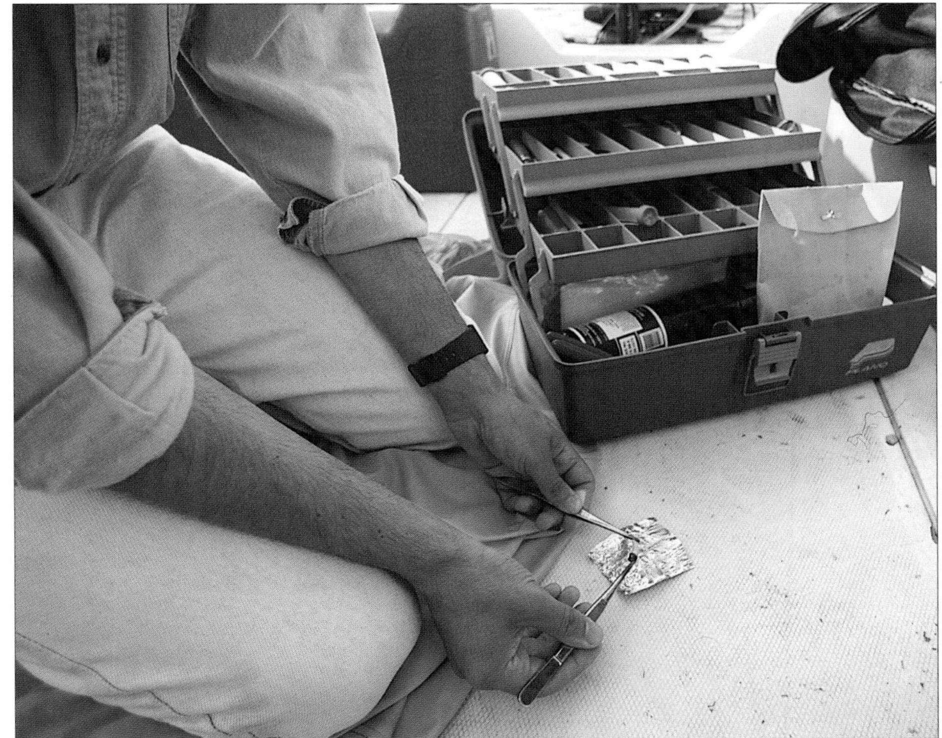

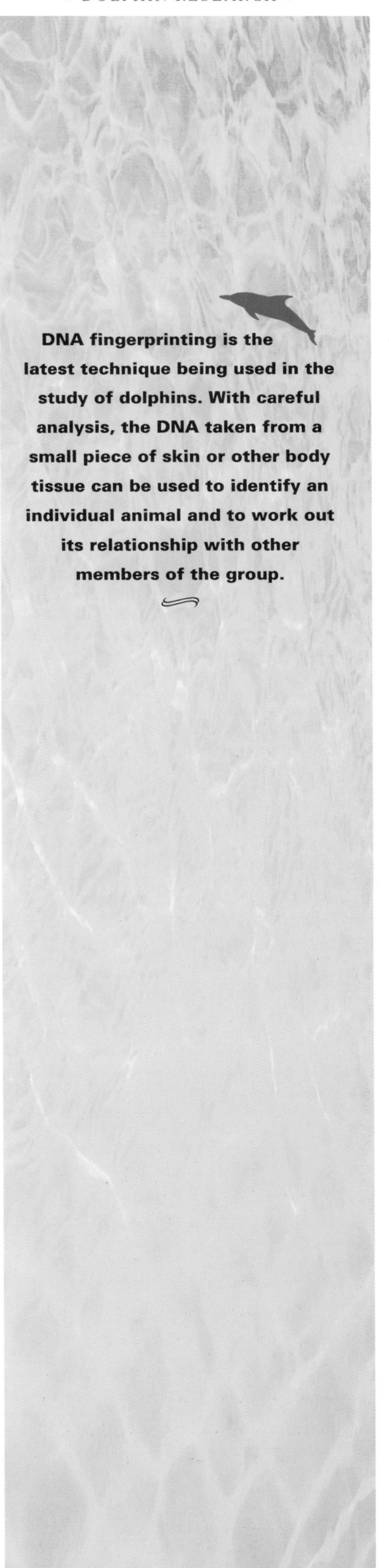

DNA fingerprinting is the latest technique being used in the study of dolphins. With careful analysis, the DNA taken from a small piece of skin or other body tissue can be used to identify an individual animal and to work out its relationship with other members of the group.

DNA Fingerprinting

Biologists are now able to use a small piece of skin or other body tissue to identify an individual animal and to investigate its relationship with other members of the group, between groups within a population, and between populations within a species. They do this by examining its genetic material, or DNA, in a complex process known as DNA fingerprinting.

The DNA itself is a kind of instruction manual for the design and assembly of the body's proteins. Every cell in an animal's body contains an exact replica of this manual, and almost all the 'pages' go to making the animal what it is – a person, a cat, a dolphin, and so on. But the small number of pages that are left help to distinguish one individual from another. Just as one person's fingerprints are different from everyone else's, no two animals have exactly the same DNA. The differences are incredibly small but, with careful chemical analysis in a laboratory, it is possible to find them. Then it is a matter of clever detective work to find out exactly what those differences mean.

The key to DNA fingerprinting is that half the fingerprint originates from the mother and the other half from the father. This means that two dolphin calves with both the same mother and the same father would have extremely similar (though not identical) fingerprints; if the calves have the same mother but a different father, only half the fingerprints would be similar; distantly related animals would have some, but much less similarity; and so on.

DNA fingerprinting is rather controversial because, when wild dolphins are being studied, it involves firing a small arrow from a crossbow to take the tiny samples of skin essential for genetic analysis. Little is known about the pain it causes, or if there are any long-term effects. But there is no doubt that it is an invaluable research tool and it is already helping to answer a number of important questions. Do different calves with the same mother have the same father? Are individuals that spend a great deal of time together closely related? Do the fathers have any direct contact with their calves, or do they leave their upbringing to the females? Many more skin samples will have to be taken before the answers to these and other questions can be confirmed, but the potential for DNA fingerprinting is both immense and tremendously exciting.

CHAPTER

6

Dolphin Mysteries

We have learnt a great deal about dolphins in recent years. But there are still a great many gaps in our knowledge and, for the most part, they remain shrouded in mystery. There are no simple answers to the questions posed in this chapter, but they demonstrate why this is such an exciting time to be involved in dolphin research. We know enough to start asking the right questions, and yet the more we scrutinize dolphin behaviour and the deeper we delve into dolphins' minds, the more we realize there is yet to learn.

Atlantic spotted dolphins, The Bahamas.

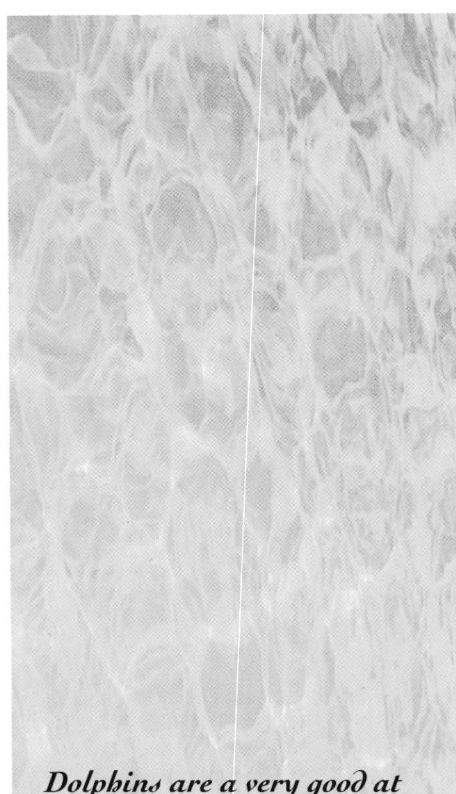

Dolphins are a very good at imitating other animals. A female bottlenose dolphin living in an oceanarium in South Africa imitated the behaviour of a fur seal in the same tank. She lay on her side with one flipper in the air, scratched herself with her flippers as if grooming — and even pretended to be a sleeping fur seal by swimming on her back with her flippers pressed flat against her chest.

How Intelligent is a Dolphin?

It is a popular notion that dolphins are as intelligent as humans. It is certainly appealing, even comforting, to imagine sharing the planet with an equally intelligent form of life – the possibilities for mutual cooperation are endless. But are dolphins really as intelligent as we would like to believe?

Many people unquestioningly accept their intelligence as gospel, while others go so far as to say that dolphins may even be our intellectual superiors. Certainly, there seems to be plenty of circumstantial evidence to support such a claim. Dolphins do have large brains; they live in complex societies; they help one another in times of trouble, even at personal risk to themselves; they rapidly learn tasks set for them under controlled conditions; they are playful and appear to have a sense of humour; and they even seem to enjoy human company.

But many of these characteristics have little to do with true intelligence. Rats, dogs, parrots, pigeons and a variety of other animals can be taught surprisingly complex tricks or tasks, for example, yet we do not assume that they are particularly intelligent. And there is no reason why we should interpret many of the tricks and tasks performed by dolphins any differently. In fact, dolphins frequently do apparently unintelligent things, such as beaching themselves and getting trapped in fishing nets.

The main confusion lies in defining what we mean by 'intelligent'. After all, we have only a human perspective, and can scarcely imagine what goes on inside another animal's mind. By 'intelligent', do we mean that the creature is perfectly adapted to its particular way of life? That it understands what it is doing and has some kind of self-awareness? Or, simply, that it shares certain characteristics with ourselves? Many definitions of intelligence have been proposed over the years but, strictly speaking, it is the ability to learn from experience and thereby to analyse new situations rather than simply react to them. Intelligent animals are able to *solve* problems by grasping fundamental principles and by making considered judgements about the possible consequences of their actions. This goes well beyond purely instinctive responses, which involve little more than fumbling around trying to get things right by trial and error.

There is plenty of circumstantial evidence to suggest that dolphins are indeed able to learn from experience and that they use reason to solve problems. In the tuna fishing areas of the Eastern Tropical Pacific (ETP), for example, dolphins with little experience of fishing operations tend to panic when they are trapped inside the nets. But in heavily fished areas, where they are more 'street-wise', they frequently wait patiently in the knowledge that they will eventually be released. In a similar vein, there have been reports of bottlenose dolphins undoing the knots that fishermen tie in their nets; even if they are pulling with no set pattern, this at least demonstrates that they understand how the nets are held together.

However, even with a working definition of intelligence, obtaining accurate measurements of these qualities in dolphins is almost impossible. There are now many different ways of assessing intellectual ability in humans, but the results can still be frustratingly ambiguous or even questionable. And since these tests usually require the use of a complex language, and an ability to work with tools such as pens or computers, measuring intelligence in other animals is even more difficult.

Studies on dolphin intelligence are following two main avenues of research. The first involves a detailed investigation into the size and structure of the brain and concentrates, in particular, on the development of the parts

responsible for learning; the second is investigating the dolphin's ability, under both wild and captive conditions, to learn from experience.

Brain size alone would suggest that some dolphins, at least, are highly intelligent. But unfortunately, this reveals little about either the nature or the extent of their intelligence. Firstly, there is a general trend for brain size to increase with body size and, of course, large animals are not necessarily more intelligent than small ones. Secondly, a major part of the brain is needed to control hearing, sight, muscular activity and a wide range of other non-intellectual functions.

A more useful measurement is the size of the brain as a percentage of the total body weight, which in dolphins varies from 0.25 to 1.5 per cent, depending on the species. This compares with a figure of 1.9 per cent in humans, and is significantly higher than in other mammals. But there are many possible reasons why dolphins have a relatively large brain – which may have nothing at all to do with intelligence. It could be required for processing complex sound information, constantly being received while they are echolocating, or even for the demands of social living. Alternatively, there is an interesting theory that it could be needed because dolphins never fall into a

Most people unquestioningly accept that dolphins are intelligent but, so far, research results are inconclusive. Some experts claim that they are at least as intelligent as humans, while others say that they are probably not as intelligent as we would like to believe.

Intelligence is notoriously difficult to study and measure in humans, let alone in dolphins, and it is important not to judge other species by our own standards.

deep sleep – they may therefore require a much larger storage area in their brain for all the unwanted information that other mammals can eliminate while they are dreaming.

An even better indication of intelligence is the development of the cerebrum. This is the region of the brain responsible for remembering the past, anticipating the future, understanding a language, rational thought, memory and the voluntary control of movements. In humans, the cerebrum is bigger than all the other parts of the brain put together. The surface of the cerebrum is intricately folded, and consists of an outer layer of nerve cell bodies (known as the cerebral cortex or, more popularly, the grey matter) and an inner mass of nerve fibres (known as the white matter). The size of the cerebral cortex, and the amount of folding, are believed to relate directly to the degree of intelligence. In some dolphins, it is more deeply folded than in humans but, confusingly, it is also relatively thin and significantly smaller overall.

The problem with comparing dolphins with humans in this way is that any discussion of relative intelligence is highly subjective. Many would call it little more than romantic speculation. Even by saying that a dolphin is more intelligent than, say, a rat or a chicken, we impose a very egocentric set of values and rules.

The simple fact that dolphins have embarked on a completely different evolutionary path from our own makes any comparison almost impossible. Human intelligence suits human needs and, consequently, a large part of our brain deals with the use of hands to write, paint, sculpt, build or manipulate objects which exist outside our own bodies. If we were to judge dolphins on these terms, they would certainly fare badly. But dolphin intelligence suits a completely different way of life, and may concentrate instead on social skills,

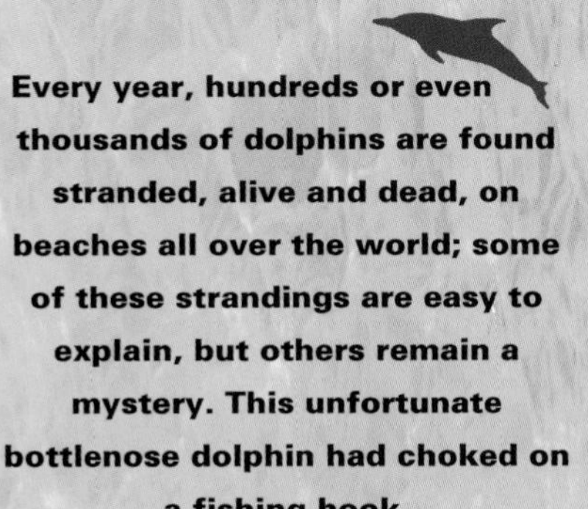

Every year, hundreds or even thousands of dolphins are found stranded, alive and dead, on beaches all over the world; some of these strandings are easy to explain, but others remain a mystery. This unfortunate bottlenose dolphin had choked on a fishing hook.

emotional self-control and other more spiritual or philosophical requirements. Many would argue that, taking this into consideration, dolphins are far more intelligent in their world than we are in ours.

Douglas Adams, in his best-selling book *The Hitch-Hiker's Guide to the Galaxy*, makes an astute observation on this very point: '...man had always assumed that he was more intelligent than dolphins because he had achieved so much – the wheel, New York, wars and so on – whilst all the dolphins had ever done was muck about in the water having a good time. But conversely, the dolphins had always believed that they were far more intelligent than man – for precisely the same reasons.'

We may never fully understand the workings of the dolphin mind – or we may simply be looking in the wrong direction. But perhaps, if we can overcome the need to compare their intelligence with our own, we may learn more by simply appreciating them for what they really are.

Why Do Dolphins Strand on Beaches?

Every year, hundreds or even thousands of dolphins are found stranded, alive and dead, on beaches all over the world. They may be alone or in groups, and while some animals are old or unwell, many of them are perfectly healthy. This is basically a natural phenomenon and, as far as we know, it has been happening since time immemorial. But it remains one of the greatest unsolved mysteries of the animal kingdom.

Recent research suggests that, in many strandings, several different factors may be at work simultaneously. However, there is still no agreement over their identity and, although there are many theories, there could well be other causes yet to be considered.

Dolphins are believed to have an extra sense, for detecting 'geomagnetism', which would enable them to 'read' the earth's magnetic field like an invisible map. It has been suggested that they could mistakenly swim onto shore after misinterpreting this map or being misled by variations in the magnetic field.

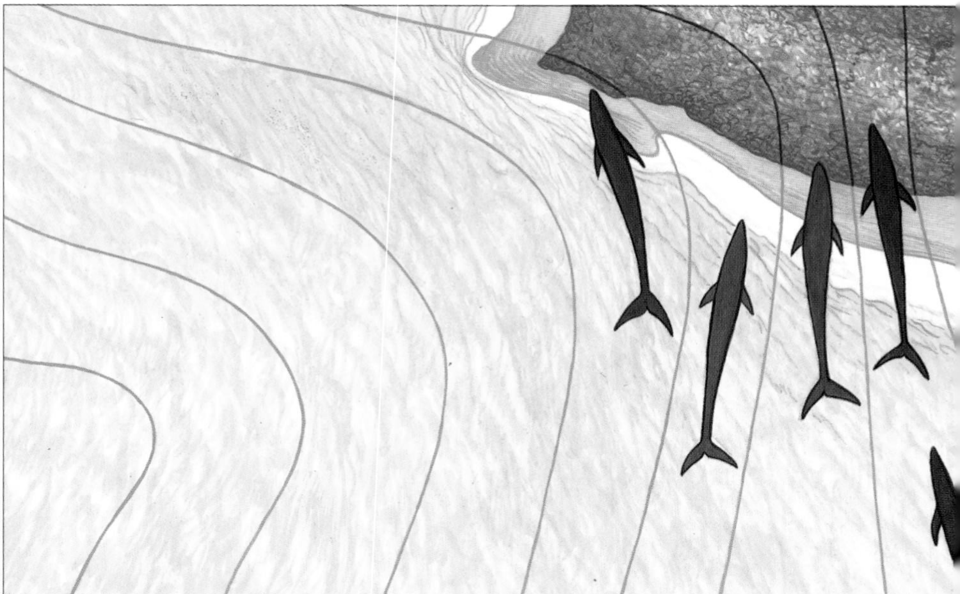

Single strandings are relatively easy to explain. In many cases, the animals simply die at sea and are washed ashore with the tides, currents and winds. Most carcasses, of course, are eaten by scavengers or decompose and sink, never to be seen again, but it is inevitable that at least some of them reach a coastline. When a single dolphin strands alive, it tends to be the result of illness or injury. In particular, dolphins suffer from a great many internal parasites, including nematodes, trematodes, hook worms, lung mites, tapeworms and a variety of others. Some infect the inner ear, for example, and could cause disorientation. Others burrow into the heart, kidney and lungs, ultimately causing such unbearable pain that the dolphin has to rest in the shallows to cope.

Mass strandings Mass strandings are far more mysterious. Even if a group of animals were all to die at the same time, for example as a result of poisoning, the vagaries of the tides, currents and winds would normally scatter their bodies over a wide area. The chances of them all washing ashore at exactly the same location are slim and, indeed, this is an extremely rare occurrence.

Mass strandings of live animals are also less common than single strandings, although they inevitably receive a great deal of media attention. They do not generally pose a threat to the species as a whole, because the numbers involved are relatively small, but dozens of thrashing and squealing dolphins floundering helplessly on a beach is a difficult welfare problem. It is certainly a haunting and distressing sight. Some species seem to be more susceptible than others. The most commonly stranded are those normally living in deep water and in large, tightly-knit social groups; their tight social cohesion is believed to explain why all the animals, rather than just a few, tend to come ashore together.

It has been suggested that mass strandings are deliberate, with the dolphins seeking somewhere to rest, hiding from sea-based predators, or even taking part in mass suicide bids. These theories seem unlikely, and the majority of experts believe that most strandings are accidental. Again, there are many different theories offered by way of explanation. One possibility is that noise or disturbance from ships, pollution, TV and radio transmissions, radar, earthquakes, storms and even phases of the Moon upset them. Another is that open ocean species may enter shallow water (after chasing fish, sheltering from severe storms or for other reasons) and then become confused. If they are near a gently sloping beach, for example, there would be a lack of echoes and

they could remain unaware of the potential danger until it is too late. Alternatively, one member of a school could be ill, and needs to rest in the shallows, and the others refuse to leave its side; when the tide goes out, they are all left stranded.

The latest theory concerns errors in navigation. Dolphins are believed to be able to 'read' the earth's magnetic field like an invisible map, and then use the geomagnetic contours like pathways across the world's seas and oceans. In the featureless marine environment, where there is normally a complete absence of physical features, the contours form invaluable hills, valleys and plains. But the magnetic field is continually fluctuating – and sometimes forms coastal 'traps' where it intersects land rather than running parallel to it. The theory suggests that dolphins could misread the information or faithfully follow the pathways onto shore. There is limited evidence from Britain and the east coast of America to suggest a link between the sites of some live strandings and local magnetic field lines, although an extensive study in New Zealand found no such link. This theory would explain why offshore species strand more often than coastal species. It would also explain why they frequently re-strand in exactly the same place, even when they have been returned to the sea by local people: they are simply putting their trust in a system that had, until then, always served them well.

Strandings are often very stressful – for both the dolphins and human observers – but they can provide scientists with a wealth of useful information. This in no way warrants the killing of animals intentionally but, by asking the right questions, it is surprising how much can be deduced from animals which strand and then die. Careful examination of the teeth, skin, blubber, muscle, bones and internal organs can provide a revealing insight into the life – and death – of the animal concerned.

What to Do if You Find a Stranded Dolphin

In most cases, a stranded dolphin will be unable to return to the sea without help. If you find one, inform the local police – who will call in the necessary experts. In some countries, especially where live strandings are frequent, volunteers are on-call twenty-four hours a day, and can respond quickly and efficiently. In others, local vets are often asked to help.

Check to see if the animal is alive, by listening for signs of breathing and looking to see if its eyes move. If it is dead, do not touch the carcass – leave it for the experts to remove. Even if it is alive, it is better to leave it to the experts if at all possible. Handled badly, a rescue attempt can cause considerable stress, and can easily result in the death of the animal. It can also be quite dangerous, since a dolphin is capable of causing serious injury if it thrashes around, and there is a danger of it passing on infection.

If expert help is likely to be a long time coming, it may be possible to make the dolphin more comfortable. The guidelines below are very basic, and should be used as a last resort.

Every stranding is different, and will demand its own solution. Whether to attempt a rescue or to humanely destroy the animals will depend on the number and size of the individuals involved, their health, the availability of lifting gear and many other factors. This difficult decision should always be made by a qualified expert. Never, under any circumstances, attempt to destroy the animals yourself.

WHAT TO DO:

- **Get expert help (via the local police) as quickly as possible.**
- **Keep the animal's skin moist with seawater.**
- **Erect a shelter to provide shade.**
- **Keep the flippers and flukes cool.**
- **Keep onlookers and their dogs at a distance to reduce stress.**
- **Make as little noise as possible.**
- **Try to keep the animal upper side up.**
- **Try to find time to take photos and make notes.**

WHAT NOT TO DO:

- **Do not stand very close to the tail or head.**
- **Do not push or pull on the flippers, flukes, or head.**
- **Do not cover the blowhole.**
- **Do not let either water or sand enter the blowhole.**
- **Do not apply suntan lotion to the animal's skin.**
- **Do not touch the animal more than necessary.**

Risso's dolphins are frequently covered in white scratches and scars, which are usually caused by the teeth of other Risso's dolphins – and give them a distinctly battered appearance.

Are Dolphins Always Unselfish and Good-natured?

The traditional image of the dolphin is of a gentle, easy-going, friendly, peaceful animal. Its social behaviour and lifestyle seem to embody many of the virtues and qualities we humans hold so dear. In fact, many people see dolphin society as closer to the human ideals of Utopia than anything we have managed to achieve on land. But while in some respects this is true and, in human terms, dolphins do indeed possess a variety of endearing qualities, it is by no means the entire story. They can become aggressive when provoked and, just like other social animals, they do have their conflicts and disagreements.

Most conflicts are resolved with the help of threat displays, and rarely end in serious physical injury. An irate dolphin opens its mouth, claps its jaws or nods its head (natural behaviours that are frequently used in entirely the wrong context during shows in marine parks) and all three displays together are a sure indication that the tension is mounting. Lobtailing, or tail slapping, may also be a sign of irritation. But if these displays do not produce the desired results, and the dolphins continue to be provoked or frustrated, they may do battle. They chase and ram each other, slap with their flukes, and rake with their teeth. Many dolphins have a labyrinth of scratches and scars on their bodies to prove the point.

The amount of aggression varies between species and, as with people, is related to the general level of stress within the population. The trauma of being confined in small concrete tanks may encourage captive dolphins to behave out of

character, while in the wild, increased boat traffic, pollution, oil or gas exploration and other forms of severe habitat disturbance may have a similar effect.

The level of aggression also varies from one individual to another. Dolphins have their own unique personalities – some are rather short-tempered, while others are more tolerant and eager to please. This is perfectly illustrated by the experiences of Ric O'Barry, who trained Flipper for the famous TV series of the same name (he has since spent his time campaigning against the captivity of dolphins). Six bottlenose dolphins were actually used for the part and, in his book *Behind the Dolphin Smile*, O'Barry mentions one particular individual called Patty. Unfortunately, Patty did not enjoy filming and, unlike the others, was bad-tempered and belligerent for much of the time. She would rush at people in the water (actors included) trying to give them a fright and generally demonstrating her displeasure. One day, O'Barry decided to teach her a lesson and, as she swam past, gave her a thump on the back. With no immediate reaction, she continued swimming to the other side of the pool, turned slowly, and then accelerated and went for O'Barry like a rocket. The next thing he knew, he was coming round with concussion in the local hospital.

'Friendly' dolphins in the wild have been known to put up with an extraordinary amount of teasing and abuse from people interacting with them in the water, frequently responding by swimming away or simply 'turning the other cheek'. But even they have their limits. An extreme case occurred in December 1994, in Brazil, when one man died and another was injured after being attacked by a male bottlenose dolphin called Tiao at a beach near Sao Paulo. Tiao had been amazingly tolerant for many months, putting up with crowds of people jumping onto his back, tying things to his flippers, pushing objects into his blowhole and even attempting to drag him out of the water onto the beach. According to onlookers, the two men had been tormenting him badly, and it seems Tiao eventually decided to retaliate.

The permanent smile of the bottlenose dolphin, and many other members of the family, is an expression that cannot be changed; dolphins continue to smile when they are feeling aggressive, when they are in intense pain, and even after death.

Dolphins have a Disney-like image as peaceful and easy-going creatures. Certainly, they engage in cooperative and 'friendly' behaviour but, like other social animals, they still have their disagreements and conflicts.

Recent research has revealed a darker side to the dolphin's nature. During 1991–93, more than forty dead harbour porpoises were found washed ashore in the Moray Firth, north-east Scotland. Their rib-cages had been crushed, some of their vital organs had been ruptured and many of them were covered in cuts and scratches. The cuts and scratches matched the teeth of local bottlenose dolphins and, although few people could believe it possible, all the evidence pointed to the fact that dolphins were the killers. Then a local man captured an actual attack on film and similar incidents have been recorded since. It seems that the dolphins play with the porpoises, in the same way that killer whales play with seals, and it takes up to forty-five minutes for their unfortunate victims to die.

It is hard to explain the ferocity of these attacks. The dolphins do not eat the porpoises, so they cannot be killing them for food. Since both species feed on fish, octopus and squid, it is just possible that they are trying to eliminate potential competitors, although this seems rather unlikely. An equally unlikely theory is that they would normally attack sharks, their main predators, and attacks on porpoises are merely cases of mistaken identity. Alternatively, as some people claim, this may not be a natural behaviour at all, and just a handful of 'rogue' dolphins may be involved in the attacks. This also seems unlikely, because there have been isolated incidents of dolphins attacking porpoises off the coast of British Columbia and in other parts of the Pacific. On the other hand, if it were a common occurrence, it seems strange that it has not been observed more often and in other parts of the world.

Dolphins frequently play with pieces of seaweed, pebbles, and other objects in the sea, carrying them around in their mouths or pushing them with their flippers.

Even well-known examples of dolphins on their best behaviour can be rather deceptive. The fact that, in times of trouble, they are always available to lend a helping hand is often quoted as proof of their selfless devotion to one another. They even come to the aid of people in distress. But in many cases such an interpretation is probably just wishful thinking – a case of attributing human emotions to another species. There is considerable evidence that care-giving is a deeply embedded instinct, with clear survival value for both the individual and the species as a whole, and that it is triggered by the presence of any dolphin-sized animal in obvious distress. It could be an injured dolphin, a human swimmer, a dead shark, or even a plank of wood.

This does not diminish the assistance provided by the dolphin, which is often at great personal risk, and it does not explain why they frequently carry people to shore rather than out to sea. It merely recognizes the fact that, in any animal, there is usually a logical explanation for such altruistic behaviour. Altruism is a survival strategy that has evolved independently in a variety of group-living animals, including some birds and social insects, and it does have significant advantages. An apparently selfless act will almost always benefit the helper in the long term: a case of 'you scratch my back and I'll scratch yours'. A female dolphin acting as a midwife while another gives birth, for example, can expect the same favour in return at a later date. There is also a good chance that the animal receiving help is in some way related to the helper – and therefore carries some of the same genes. This gene theory is supported by recent research, which suggests that assistance may be given selectively, and only in certain circumstances.

The problem with a brief overview of this kind is that it tends to paint an unnecessarily black picture of the dolphin. But dolphins are no different to many other animals and, if anything, delving deeper into their complex nature makes them even more intriguing and interesting. It certainly does not detract from their magical appeal. The critical finger should really be pointed at us – for attempting to force our own emotions and ideals onto another species.

Do Dolphins Really Play?

Play is one of the most complicated forms of animal behaviour and, although it is often discussed in relation to dolphins, it is still a rather controversial subject. The problem is that no-one can agree on whether certain activities are purely for pleasure, or if they have a greater purpose.

Dolphins certainly appear to spend a considerable amount of their time playing and apparently having fun. In human terms, they exude a real sense of joyfulness. They chase one another, leap into the air, perform an astonishing variety of acrobatics, splash the water with their tails, surf on coastal breakers, and launch into sudden bursts of speed swimming. If they hear a passing ship or boat, they frequently go out of their way to ride in the bow waves or in the 'Jacuzzi' formed by the frothy wake. Many of them seem to enjoy the company of people, seals, sea turtles, and a variety of other species. They even delight in

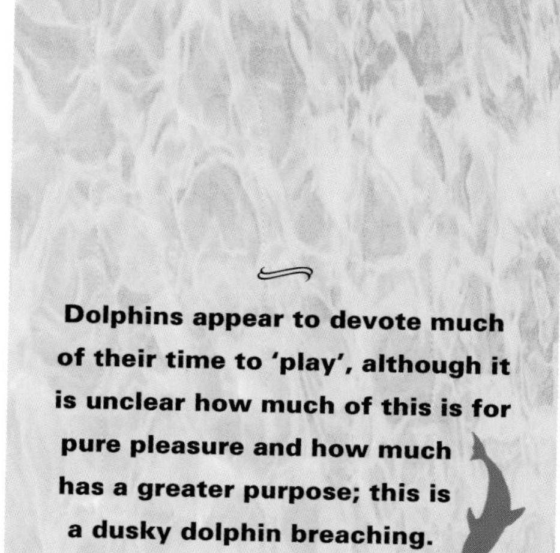

Dolphins appear to devote much of their time to 'play', although it is unclear how much of this is for pure pleasure and how much has a greater purpose; this is a dusky dolphin breaching.

long and involved games with pieces of seaweed, dead fish, pebbles, jellyfish and other objects in the sea, carrying them around in their mouths or balancing them on their flippers or fins.

Their play is often so mischievous that they frequently appear to have a real sense of humour. There are countless instances of friendly dolphins apparently amusing themselves by tugging at divers' masks, for example, to make them fill up with water; others have been known to pick up heavy anchors and tow boats away. Such pranks may also have something to do with boredom. Dolphins are efficient hunters and, when there is plenty of food around, probably have both time and energy to spare. Consider Fungie, the friendly bottlenose dolphin living in Ireland's Dingle Bay. He has been seen entertaining himself by playing with guillemots, coming up underneath one of the birds as it lands on the surface of the water and then flipping it back into the air with his beak. Then he rushes over to where the hapless guillemot is about to land back in the sea, and does it again.

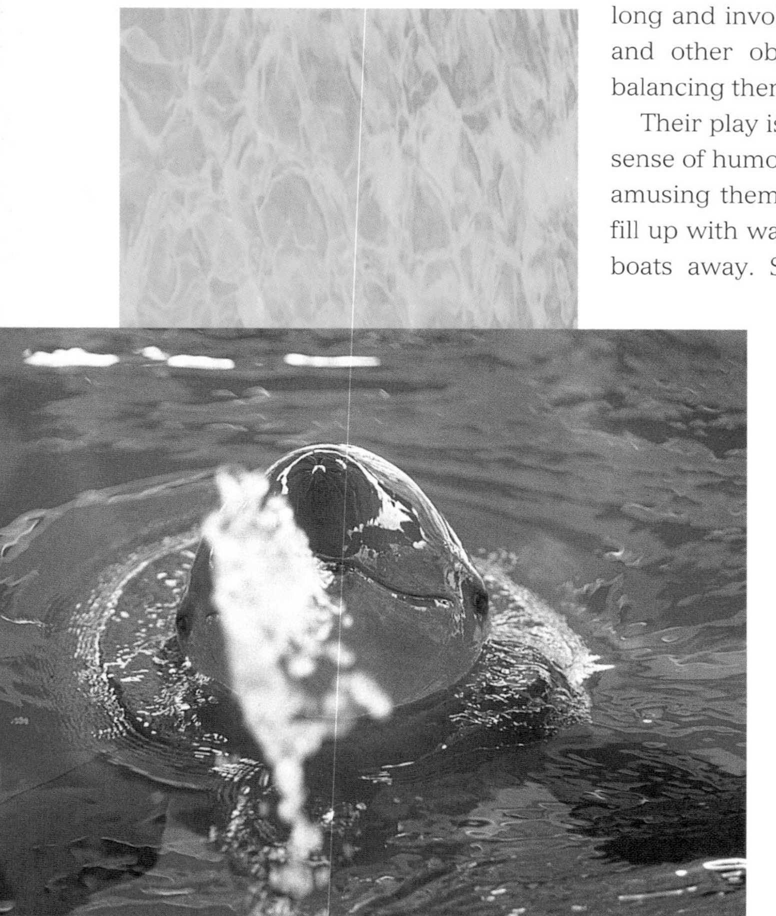

This Irrawaddy dolphin, bored with life in a small, concrete tank in a marine park near Bangkok, Thailand, kept itself amused by squirting water at unsuspecting passers-by.

Swimming in the frothy wake of a boat or ship seems to be a favourite pastime for many dolphins. They surf in the waves and, like this bottlenose dolphin, twist and turn or swim upside-down in the bubbles.

Inevitably, there are logical explanations for some of these activities. In young animals, they form part of the learning process, helping them to master different forms of behaviour that will be a vital part of their adult life. But dolphins of all ages are known to play, so this cannot be the sole explanation. In fact, some species are equal to apes – or may even surpass them – in the sheer variety of their play activities.

Recent research suggests that many of their games and acrobatics serve important functions in communication, courtship, food-herding, predator defence and other aspects of daily life. Leaping out of the water, for example, may be to look for seabirds gathering to feed on fish, while noisy splashing may scare the fish into a tight cluster ready to catch. Play for its own sake may even have a crucial role in strengthening social bonds within a group – the equivalent, in human terms, of office parties and lunchtime drinks.

Some forms of play are extremely difficult to interpret and, at the end of the day, may not have logical explanations at all. Despite all the theories and the likely advantages of play, it may not be too fanciful to suggest that dolphins sometimes indulge in certain activities for no better reason than they are good fun.

Bow-riding is a good example. Dolphins frequently jostle for the best position in front of a fast-moving boat or ship, where they can be pushed along in the water by the force of the bow-wave. Some species do it more often than others, and certain vessels are more inclined to attract bow-riding dolphins than others. Even large whales, such as the fin and blue, sometimes attract 'bow-riders' in front of their heads while they are swimming close to the sea surface. Once in position, they hold their flukes slightly up or down (depending on the type of wave) and at just the right angle to the water deflecting from the bow. Remaining in the pressure field, where there is sufficient force to be propelled forward, is difficult because the prime spot constantly shifts as the vessel pitches in the sea. If a dolphin is slightly out of position when it stops swimming it pops out of the field but, if it is well positioned, it can keep pace with the speeding vessel while barely moving a muscle.

One explanation for bow-riding – which is thrilling to watch from the bow itself – is that it is simply a way of hitching a free ride. This may be true in some cases, but certainly not all; the dolphins frequently appear to swim a considerable distance out of their way to join a vessel and then, when they have had enough, swim back to their original position. It is one of many dolphin mysteries that have enthralled scientists and seafarers alike for centuries.

CHAPTER

7

Dolphins and People

There is a sense of kinship between dolphins and people that goes back for thousands of years. It is almost as if we accept dolphins as our equals. We are desperately keen to be able to communicate with them, and eager to be accepted as their friends. A close encounter with a dolphin can be extremely emotional, and may even trigger the healing process in people who are mentally or physically unwell.

Bottlenose dolphin, Monkey Mia, Australia.

The god Apollo saw the smallest whale, the dolphin,

As the embodiment of peaceful virtue, undisguised joy

And as a guide to another world.

He sometimes exchanged his god-like status

To assume dolphin form;

And founded the oracle at Delphi,

Named in the dolphin's honour.

There, the god hoped,

Man might be guided by a sense of other-worldliness.

HEATHCOTE WILLIAMS

Dolphins in Mythology

Dolphins have played an important role in human mythology and culture for thousands of years. In fact, their involvement reaches back nearly to the beginning of civilization, and even today the 'magic' of dolphins still captures the imagination of artists and storytellers around the world.

The earliest known portrayal of dolphins and other small cetaceans in art are ancient drawings carved into rocks in northern Norway. One shows a killer whale with moose and other local wildlife, and is estimated to be some 9,000 years old; another, more than 4,000 years old, shows a man in a boat apparently hunting a seal and two porpoises. A number of others have been found in the same region, depicting several different dolphin species.

A few centuries later, early Greek and Roman artists – clearly inspired by the dolphin's intelligence and apparent kindness to humans – began to adopt dolphin motifs on vases, coins, mosaic floors, and in sculptures, paintings and drawings. One of the earliest and better-known of these is the dolphin fresco on the wall of the Queen's Room in the Minoan palace of Knossos, on the island of Crete, which was painted by an unknown artist about 3,500 years ago.

The ancient Greeks – among the first great seafarers – held dolphins in such high regard that killing them was tantamount to killing a person, and both crimes were punishable by the death penalty. The works of many classical Greek scholars, from the naturalists Aristotle and Theophrastus to the historians Plutarch and Herodotus, reveal a genuine interest in dolphins at the time, and an admiration for their trusting nature and friendliness.

It is not surprising that dolphins appear frequently in classical Greek mythology, and were closely linked with the gods. The sun god Apollo, for example, assumed the form of a dolphin when he founded his shrine or oracle at Delphi ('Dolphin Town') on the slopes of Mount Parnassus. In another Greek myth, the hero Orion was carried into the sky on the back of a dolphin and given three stars, which became the famous constellation of stars known as Orion's Belt.

It was the Greeks' respect for dolphins which probably inspired the Romans to take an interest in them too. The Roman world was captivated by the dolphin's extraordinary friendliness, its alleged passion for music and its delight in swimming around ships. But the Romans were less emotive and sentimental about nature than the Greeks, and many of their dolphin stories tended to have tragic endings.

The Roman philosopher Pliny the Elder (AD 23–79) was one of the great storytellers of his age, and wrote one of the most famous of all stories about

The ancient Greeks and Romans were captivated by dolphins; this mosaic was found in a Roman villa on the ancient site of Halicarnassus, Turkey, and is believed to be about 1,500 years old.

human–dolphin relationships. It concerned the friendship of a peasant boy and a dolphin in the Mediterranean Sea. One day, on his way to school, the boy saw a solitary dolphin and managed to coax it into the shallows to feed it some bread from his lunch box. The two quickly became firm friends. The boy called the dolphin Simo, and every day went hungry himself in order to give Simo some of his lunch. Simo would gratefully accept the offering and, in return, gave the boy a ride on his back across the bay to school. The friendship lasted for years, until the boy suddenly became ill and died. Simo continued to visit their meeting point on the beach every day but, of course, the boy never returned. As the days passed, the poor animal became sadder and sadder and, eventually, according to the locals, he died of a broken heart.

Many ancient myths and stories were based on second- or even third-hand accounts and it is therefore impossible to say how much they reflect true events and experiences. The great majority are fanciful; others could well be based on fact. It is particularly interesting that so many of them reveal an early awareness of dolphins, and a belief that they are in some way different. Also, many contained an important truth or moral – in particular, they taught the importance of respecting the natural world, and gave a warning that anyone who treated it with contempt was sure to experience the wrath of the gods.

Many ancient cultures – like the Aborigines, Maoris, Polynesians and American Indians – traditionally regard dolphins as spirits, messengers of the gods, or even human beings living in the sea. In Polynesian folklore, for example, ancestral spirits are believed to take the form of guardian dolphins, who guide canoes, rescue people in difficulty, and assist local fishermen. Many of these modern-day Polynesian stories about the friendliness of dolphins are remarkably similar to the ones appearing in classical Greek literature.

Dolphins feature prominently in the myths and folklore of most sea-faring nations – their special 'magic' has captured the imagination of writers and artists for centuries.

One of the most interesting interactions between dolphins and people, still surviving today, involves a tribe of Aborigines known as the Dolphin People. They live on Mornington Island, in the Gulf of Carpentaria, northern Australia, and are said to have been in direct communication with a nearby population of wild bottlenose dolphins for thousands of years. They believe that their fortune and happiness depend on keeping in contact with these dolphins. At their traditional ceremonies the tribal shaman, or medicine man, makes a complex series of whistles that are supposed to attract the dolphins close to shore. When the whistling stops, and the dolphins are in the shallows nearby, the shaman then begins to 'speak' to the animals by telepathy, one mind to another.

It is not uncommon for individual dolphins to befriend humans, allowing or even encouraging physical contact over a period of months or years.

So many people now visit Monkey Mia, in Western Australia, in the hope of meeting the local bottlenose dolphins, that information signs and qualified rangers are needed to ensure that the animals come to no harm.

Do Dolphins Really Enjoy Human Company?

Throughout history, there has been a deep-rooted belief that dolphins really do enjoy human company. For many people, this is undoubtedly one of the most appealing aspects of their character.

It is certainly true that some dolphins actively seek out human company and allow – or even encourage – physical contact. Over months or years, they learn to discriminate between different people (even in wetsuits underwater or clothed in a boat), and develop their own special friendships. Yet they also rescue complete strangers, helping swimmers in distress or protecting them from sharks.

Stories of dolphins herding sharks away from people are quite common. A long-distance swimmer, John Koorey, describes how a school of dolphins escorted him across New Zealand's Cook Strait. At one point, they suddenly disappeared, only to reappear a few moments later as if nothing had happened. According to observers on Koorey's safety boat, the dolphins had driven away a potentially dangerous group of sharks that were swimming around nearby. More recently, a woman was in the water with a female humpback whale and her calf off the coast of Tonga in the South Pacific, when a large bronze-whaler shark suddenly appeared. Within moments, she was surrounded by a group of spinner dolphins – and they stayed with her until the shark had lost interest and swam away.

'Friendly' Dolphins The modern image of the 'friendly' dolphin was best portrayed in the 1960s TV series *Flipper*. Whenever people were in trouble, the star of the show, a bottlenose dolphin, was always there to save the day. In real life, dolphin rescues have been reported on many occasions, and from many parts of the world. One night in November 1988, for example, two sailors were shipwrecked in rough seas off the coast of Indonesia. As soon as their ship had sunk, a group of dolphins appeared. The animals nudged and guided the two men throughout the night, until they finally reached the safety of dry land by morning.

In some cases, 'friendly' dolphins clearly benefit from their good deeds. Near the town of Laguna, in southern Brazil, wild bottlenose dolphins cooperate with thirty or forty local fishermen in a way that pays off for both parties. The fishermen stand in the shallow, murky water, poised with their circular throw nets, while a couple of dolphins station themselves a few metres

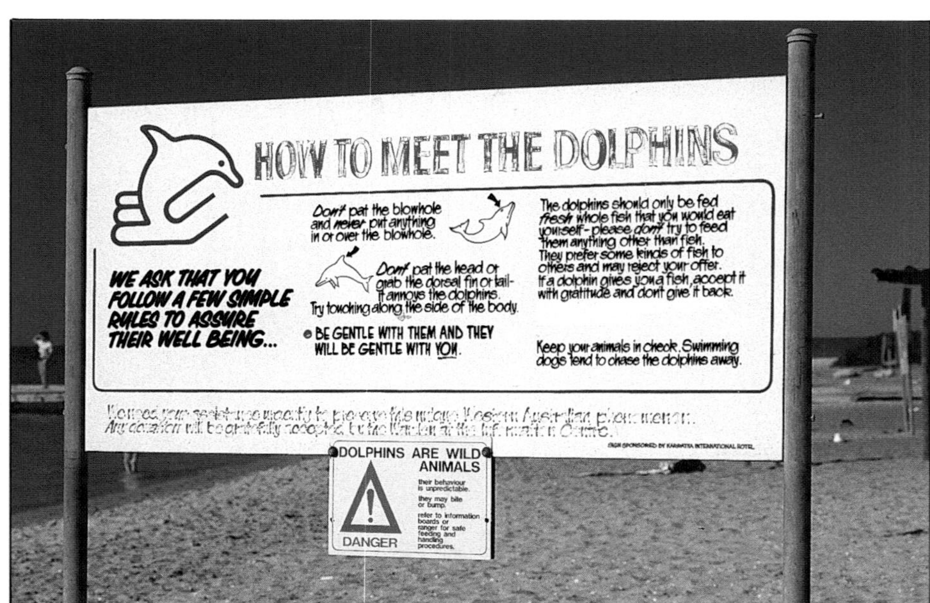

seac

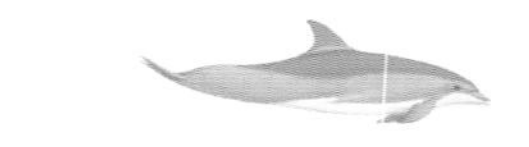

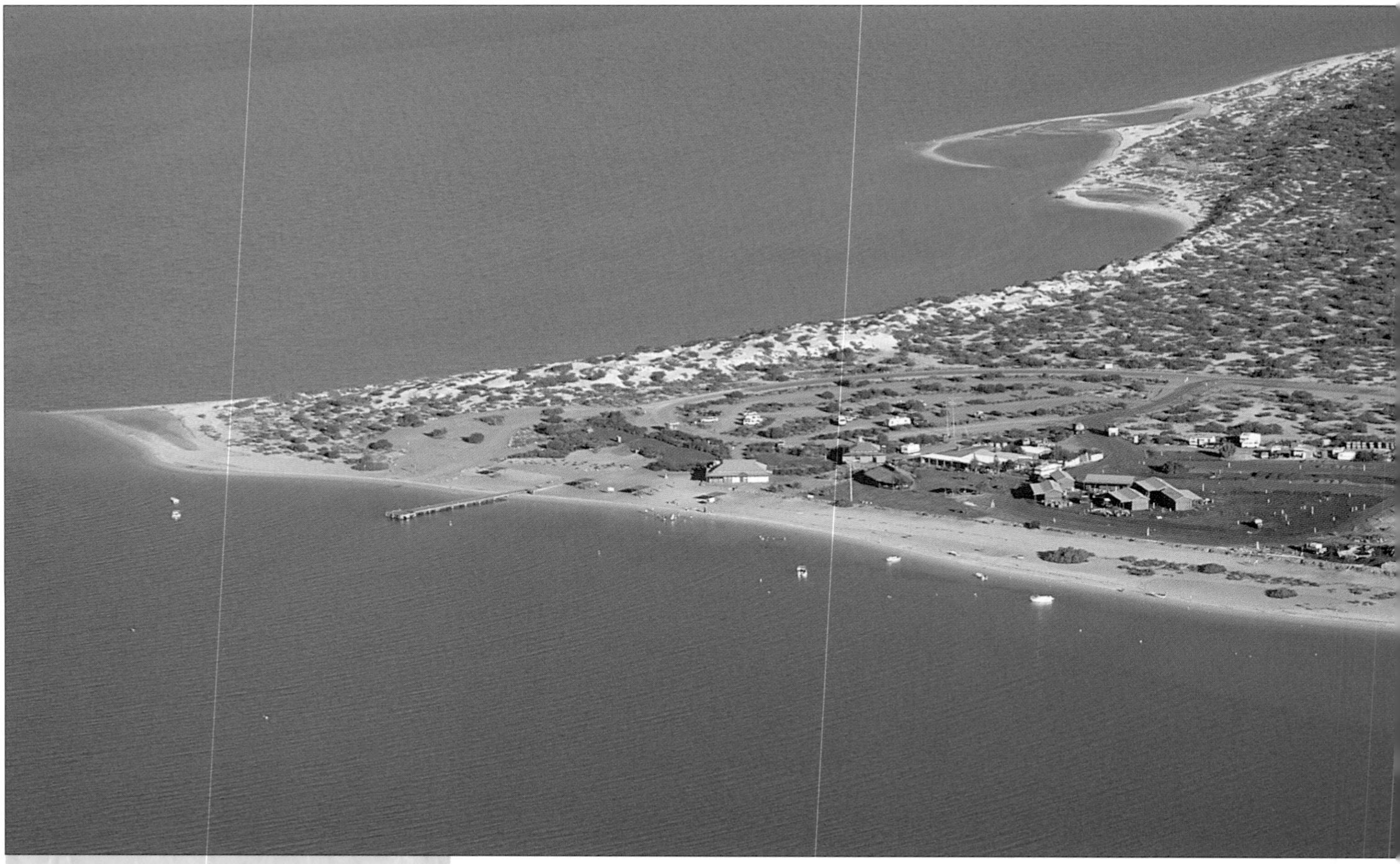

Monkey Mia, on the remote western coast of Australia, has become one of the country's leading tourist attractions: wild bottlenose dolphins have been greeting people here for more than thirty years. Unfortunately, there is now concern about the level of dependency shown by the dolphins on their human friends.

away. As soon as one of the dolphins makes an abrupt, stereotyped surface roll, the fishermen cast their nets. While they are hauling them in, the dolphins snatch any fish (normally mullet) that try to escape in all the confusion. This remarkable fishing system – initiated and controlled by the dolphins rather than the humans – has operated almost daily for over 100 years. There are similar human–dolphin fishing cooperatives in Mauritania, West Africa (with Atlantic hump-backed dolphins); south-east Queensland, Australia (with bottlenose dolphins); Burma (with Irrawaddy dolphins); and several other parts of the world.

These so-called 'friendly' dolphins capture the human imagination the most. At least ten dolphin species are known to have shown a preference for human company, although the bottlenose is easily the friendliest of them all. In the past forty years, about fifty friendlies have been reported around the world.

It is quite easy to imagine how these friendships could develop. Dolphins are incredibly inquisitive animals – some would say downright nosy – and if something attracts their attention, they find it hard to resist the temptation to investigate. The more encouragement they receive, the more likely they are to respond.

Why gregarious animals like dolphins should choose to live apart from their social groups and seek out human company instead is a complete mystery. They do not seem to be soliciting food which, after all, is why most wild animals allow people to approach them closely. If a wild dolphin is thrown a fish, it is more likely to regard it as a toy than a meal.

In most cases, friendly dolphins are solitary animals. It has been suggested that they could be outcasts – dolphin misfits that have been ostracized from their social groups. Perhaps human company offers them some comfort for being on their own? This is an intriguing theory, although it is unlikely to be correct because the dolphins appear to behave perfectly normally in every other way. In fact, recent observations suggest that some of them may still maintain a degree of social contact with other dolphins.

It is possible that some friendlies may have been separated from their social groups by accident, perhaps during storms or attacks by sharks or killer whales. Alternatively, some of them could be orphans, separated from their mothers when they are still young. Although friendly dolphins can be male or female, and of any age, they do tend to be either young or old (increasing the likelihood of them being lost or 'between schools'). It is also possible that some may have escaped or gone absent without leave while on military manoeuvres in the open sea.

In truth, there is no explanation. As dolphins are such complex characters and, like people, frequently do things their own way, they probably have reasons for seeking out human company which we may not even have considered.

'Friendlies' Around the World One of the first friendly dolphins to become an international celebrity was a Risso's dolphin named Pelorus Jack. He escorted ferry steamers through New Zealand's narrow French Pass for about twenty-four years, from 1888 until 1912. (It was always assumed that 'he' was a male – but no-one knew for sure). Pelorus Jack met an untimely death in April 1912, when he was harpooned by the crew of a Norwegian whaling boat anchored offshore. He is still fondly remembered to this day.

Over the years, it seems, New Zealand has had more friendly dolphins than many other countries. Another of its well-known friendlies was a young female bottlenose dolphin called Opo. She suddenly turned up in 1955, after a storm near Opononi, Hokianga Harbour. She spent much time swimming with bathers and playing with children in the shallows, attracting as many as 2,000 people every day. Then, on 9 March 1956, she was found dead – blown to pieces by gelignite. Ironically, it was the day after a law had been passed by the local council to give her official protection. Whether Opo had been killed on purpose or accidentally, no-one will ever know. But the grieving local community gave her a public funeral, and a statue was erected to commemorate nine months of her company.

In recent years, Britain and Ireland have also had more than their fair share of friendly dolphins, all of them bottlenose. Charlie was one of only two females: she frequented the area between Fife and Northumberland during the mid-1960s. Then there was Donald, or 'Beaky' as he was often known, who first appeared around the Isle of Man in 1972; he spent the next six years travelling south, stopping off in small harbours and coves in Wales and Cornwall, and swimming with hundreds of people along the way. Then two other dolphins appeared in the same region. First there was Percy, who lived at Portreath, Cornwall, from 1982–84. Then there was Simo, who lived around Solva, Pembrokeshire, from 1984–86. No sooner had Simo disappeared than Freddie, or 'Dougal' as he is known by some, turned up near Amble, Northumberland; he arrived in 1986, and stayed until 1992. As Freddie was leaving, another female turned up in Southampton, Hampshire, and stayed until 1993. But perhaps the most famous of all is Fungie, known to many simply as 'the Dingle dolphin'. Fungie appeared in Dingle Bay, County Kerry, for the first time in 1987, and is now one of Ireland's greatest tourist attractions.

While most friendly dolphins are alone, there are also some remarkable examples of larger groups of dolphins associating with people on a day-to-day basis. Two places are particularly well-known: Monkey Mia, on the shores of Shark Bay, in a remote corner of Western Australia; and Little Bahama Bank, north of Grand Bahama Island, in the North Atlantic.

Monkey Mia Wild bottlenose dolphins have been greeting people at Monkey Mia almost every day for more than three decades. It is now the longest-running human–dolphin encounter on record. The story began on a still night in 1964, when Alice and Ern Watts anchored their boat in Monkey Mia

'Wherever dolphins have impinged on a human mind, it seems a deep and resonant chord is struck.'

WADE DOAK
CETACEAN EXPERT

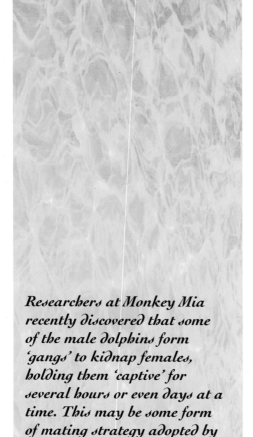

Researchers at Monkey Mia recently discovered that some of the male dolphins form 'gangs' to kidnap females, holding them 'captive' for several hours or even days at a time. This may be some form of mating strategy adopted by distraught bachelor males that have not been chosen by females as mates.

bay. It was extremely hot and, around midnight, Alice went outside for some fresh air. As she sat on the deck, a dolphin began to swim around the boat. She watched it for a while, threw it a fish from the ice-box, and went back to bed. It was the beginning of a long and happy friendship. Within a few weeks, 'Charlie' was bringing other dolphins into Monkey Mia. Before long, they were taking fish from the hands of locals who waded into the shallows to meet them.

Charlie died, but his friends continued to visit. By the time Wilf and Hazel Mason arrived to take over the ramshackle caravan park on the beach, in 1974, the dolphins and the local people were old friends. From the beginning, Wilf and Hazel established a special rapport with their new neighbours, and soon became their unofficial guardians. To their credit, they turned away all proposals to teach the dolphins tricks and commercialize them. However, word of the dolphins' friendly visits reached the outside world, and Monkey Mia gradually became one of Australia's main tourist destinations.

With the growing number of human visitors, it became obvious that some people were feeding the animals scraps of inappropriate food, or even rubbish, and others were being a little rough. So permanent wardens were employed to make sure the dolphins came to no harm.

Nowadays, more than a hundred thousand people visit Monkey Mia every year. The place itself has changed beyond all recognition. The ramshackle caravan park has grown into a modern facility, with an assortment of buildings, a store, an information centre, a jetty, and hundreds of cars and tourist buses in the car park. But still the dolphins continue to come. It does not seem to make any difference that almost all the people crowding knee-deep in 'their' water are complete strangers.

Several times a day, most days, as many as ten or twelve dolphins make the pilgrimage to Monkey Mia beach. They belong to a much larger group of dolphins living offshore but, intriguingly, are the only ones to seek close human contact. All the visiting dolphins are different. Some are placid and unruffled by almost anything; others have been known to get a little aggressive with anyone who frightens or provokes them. They swim between people's legs, wait to be scratched or tickled, and play catch with pieces of seaweed or fish. Sometimes, they beach themselves in no more than a few inches of water and simply watch the crowds gathered to see them. It is often hard to tell who is supposed to be watching whom. It is even harder to believe that they are really wild dolphins, visiting the beach on their own terms. Not only do they choose to come, but they also bring their calves with them – as if to carry on the tradition.

In recent years, Monkey Mia has caused considerable concern. Since the dolphins are being fed (a practice which is illegal in many other parts of the world), it seems that females with calves are spending too much time at the beach and not enough time teaching their calves how to catch prey – or defending them from sharks. As a result, there seems to be a higher juvenile mortality rate than in other bottlenose dolphin populations.

Little Bahama Bank Little Bahama Bank is quite different to Monkey Mia, but no less intriguing. Many miles from the nearest land, it is a shallow bank (only 9–12 metres [30–40 feet] deep) with crystal-clear water and a brilliant-white sandy bottom. More importantly, it is the home of a friendly population of Atlantic spotted dolphins. The dolphins genuinely seem to enjoy human company, and are now attracting small groups of tourists from all over the world.

As Little Bahama Bank covers quite a large area, finding the dolphins can take several days. But all the time and effort is amply rewarded within a few moments of the first close encounter. There is nothing else quite like it in the world. Sometimes, it is possible to be surrounded by dozens of inquisitive and

playful dolphins for minutes or even hours at a time. Other times, there may be only a few that watch or copy your every move. They can be a little nervous of scuba divers, but frequently come to within an arm's length of snorkellers. They swim alongside, dive underneath, race backwards and forwards, twist and spiral, performing the most amazing slow-motion ballets. Even females with their calves come to see what is going on, swimming next to one another and often touching flipper-to-flipper, like a mother and child holding hands.

Denise Herzing, who has studied the Bahamian dolphins for many years, has probably had more underwater encounters with them than anyone else. She describes a remarkable occasion when a human mother entered the water with her baby. One particular dolphin watched the youngster very closely, and then swam off. Minutes later it returned – with a calf of its own.

Anyone who has swum with the dolphins of Little Bahama Bank, witnessed the daily get-togethers at Monkey Mia, or been in the water with a lone friendly dolphin, could have no doubt that many dolphins really do enjoy human company. It seems that some may even prefer being with humans to socializing with other dolphins. But they are the exception, not the rule. In some parts of the world, especially where there is heavy hunting or fishing, many dolphins go out of their way to avoid close contact with people. Others will readily approach boats, but are nervous of people in the water. After all, who can blame them? They are not always treated with the respect they deserve.

The wild bottlenose dolphins of Monkey Mia enthusiastically 'strand' themselves on a daily basis to be fed, petted and admired by complete strangers.

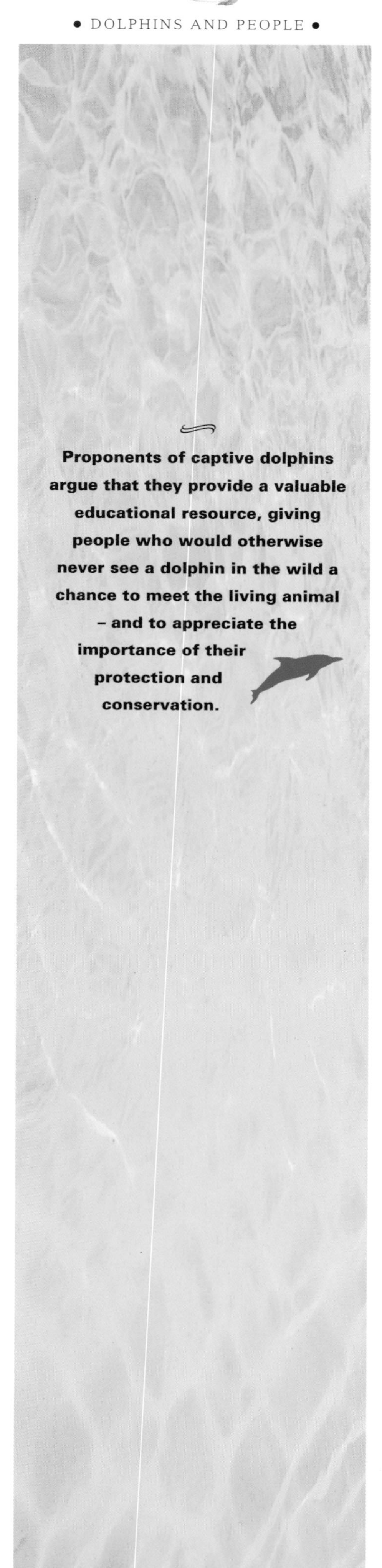

Proponents of captive dolphins argue that they provide a valuable educational resource, giving people who would otherwise never see a dolphin in the wild a chance to meet the living animal – and to appreciate the importance of their protection and conservation.

Dolphins in Captivity

Wild dolphins have been captured and kept in captivity for more than a century. Most of them are trained to perform special shows for the fee-paying public and are put on display purely for financial profit. The rest are kept for research purposes or are used by the military. Their plight has become a highly controversial issue in recent years, stirring really powerful emotions in many people. The big question is whether or not keeping a relatively small number of dolphins in captivity, albeit for financial gain, can be justified by the educational and research spin-offs that are claimed could benefit their wild relatives.

There is no doubt that captive dolphins are immensely popular. Millions of people flock to see them every year, and they are the undisputed stars of marine parks and aquariums around the world. They are worth a lot of money. They

directly or indirectly provide thousands of people with secure jobs and, at the same time, make a select few very rich. Dolphins themselves could benefit in the long run, if the captives can effectively act as 'ambassadors' to encourage people to take an interest in the plight of their wild relatives, and if they are studied for the greater benefit of all. However, animal welfare groups on several continents maintain that it is immoral and cruel to keep dolphins in small tanks and pools, and claim that the potential spin-offs have been grossly exaggerated. Many of them are now campaigning for the capture of wild dolphins to be banned and for existing captive dolphins to be released.

The first attempts to capture and exhibit dolphins date back to the early 1860s, although there was little success in those early days. Capturing dolphins without injury, minimizing the stress they inevitably suffer during transport, and encouraging them to adapt to their new confined homes proved to be

The bottlenose dolphin shows a more striking range in size between individuals than any other dolphin species. Physically mature adults vary in length from just under 2 metres (6 1/4 feet) to nearly four metres (12 3/4 feet) and in weight from 150 kg (330 lbs) to 650 kg (1,430 lbs).

more difficult than many people had realized. A great many dolphins died from shock in the first few hours or days, and the remainder rarely survived more than a few months. It took years of trial and error, and the unfortunate loss of many animals, before anyone really began to understand their requirements.

During the 1970s, the number of facilities for captive dolphins increased dramatically throughout North America, Europe, Japan and parts of south-east Asia. Many of them still exist today, and new facilities continue to swell their ranks. Between them, they have attempted to keep at least twenty dolphin species. The most common has always been the bottlenose, which can be caught along many coastlines and adapts *relatively* well to captive conditions. Many thousands of small cetaceans have been captured alive for display (or research) purposes over the years and, although a small number are now being bred in captivity, they are still being taken from the wild.

Capture techniques vary. Dolphins living close to shore are normally driven into shallow water. Others are caught as they ride the bow-waves of the capture boat; a net is placed over their heads, then a diver manoeuvres them into slings ready to be hoisted on board.

The Problems of Tank Life The transition from life in the open sea to confinement in a small tank or pool can be extremely traumatic. Some facilities are obviously much better than others, but in the worst scenario, the captive dolphin has nowhere to go in its bare and featureless home. It can no longer hunt or hear the sounds of the sea, is unable to dive into the murky depths and may even be deprived of natural sunlight. It has to acclimatize to a diet of dead fish, the presence of noisy human observers and a severe lack of familiar company. Even if it is with other dolphins, an individual that was dominant in the open sea may not have the same leadership role in the tank, and a shy animal cannot escape from an aggressive one. It may also have to share its new home with several species in a grouping that would seldom, if ever, exist in the wild.

The water in the tank can be a source of endless health problems, adding to these stresses. Its pH level, salinity, temperature and other important variables have to be monitored regularly, and there is often a deluge of rubbish that needs to be filtered and removed. A bottlenose dolphin can produce 1.4 kg (3 lb) of faeces and 4 litres (7 pints) of urine a day, as well as moulted skin and the remains of previous meals. Also, many tanks seem to act as magnets for everything from blown leaves to sweet wrappers, which exacerbates the problem. Some badly managed marine parks and aquariums rarely bother to clear the mess.

It is not surprising that the permanent 'smiles' of many captive dolphins often hide an inner suffering. Dolphins are as likely to suffer from psychological disorders as other zoo animals. A small number do adjust to life in a tank and, with professional care and attention, eventually seem to accept their new homes, although whether or not they are 'happy' is another matter altogether. Some even breed in captivity and, once they reach adulthood, have life expectancies that are comparable to those of their wild relatives or better, but others simply cannot cope. They repeatedly circle their small tanks, develop stereotyped behaviour, stop vocalizing, become aggressive, get depressed, and often die prematurely. A few inflict injuries upon themselves, and some have committed suicide by banging their heads against the tank walls.

The better holding facilities have solved some of these fundamental problems. The best of them keep their dolphins in carefully structured family groups in large netted enclosures on the coast. Several acres in size, and deep enough for swimming and diving, these enclosures bear little resemblance to the more traditional concrete tanks. They are filled naturally with sea water, and flushed with every new tide. The dolphins are fed a varied selection of fish, as well as

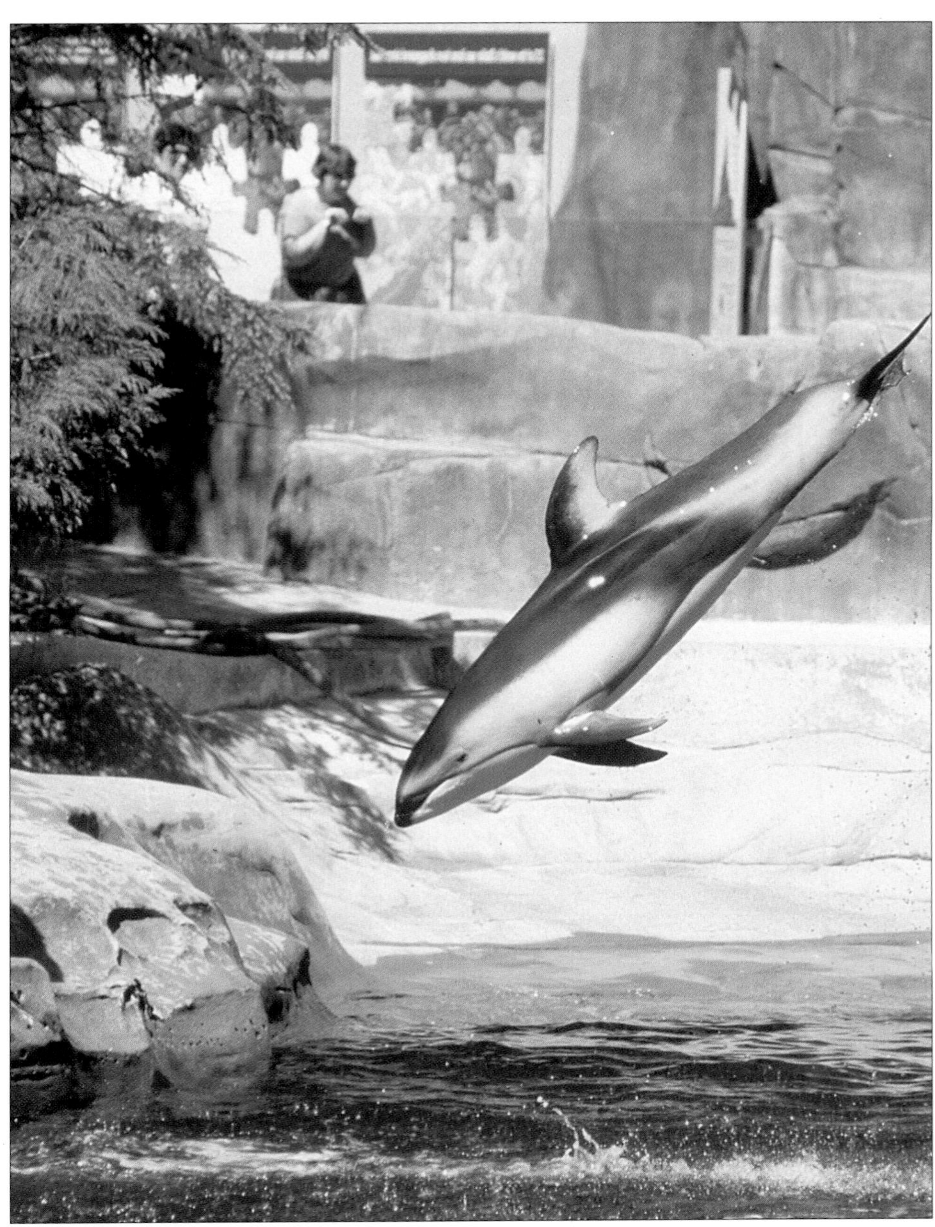

Critics of captive dolphins often point to the degrading nature of dolphin shows and to the traumas of living imprisoned in small tanks.

vitamin and mineral supplements, and have regular check-ups by experienced vets. Health problems are quickly treated with medication, food supplements and, of course, extra care and attention by their trainers. The argument for these more professional facilities is that captivity is a simple trade-off; the animals give up their freedom and natural companions in return for escaping the two biggest problems of life in the wild: going hungry and getting eaten.

Dolphin Shows Whether it is a small tank or a large netted enclosure, most animal welfare groups condemn any captive facility that trains its dolphins to perform 'tricks'. The animals are often obliged to participate in public shows several times every day – 'kissing' their trainers, somersaulting, jumping through hoops, fetching balls and performing synchronized leaps. These are the result of much hard work – and can take weeks, or even months, to prepare.

The tricks are usually based on natural behaviours; the dolphins are simply trained to perform them on command. In the early days, some trainers meted out punishments in the form of electric shocks, but they soon discovered that progress was hindered rather than helped if the dolphins were penalized every time they did something wrong. Nowadays, the basic concept of training is

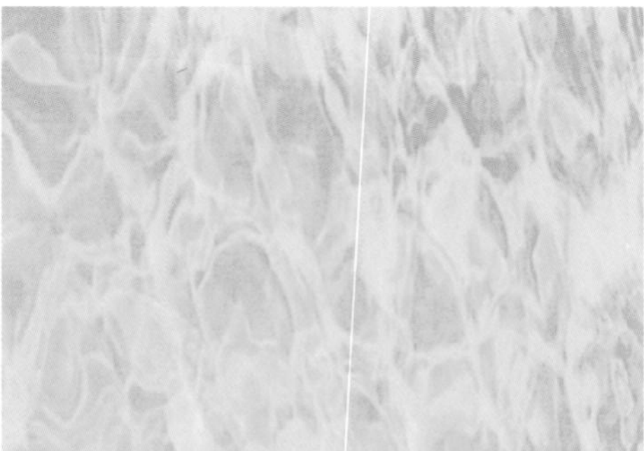

normally positive reinforcement. The dolphins are given food rewards or encouraging 'pats on the back' for doing well. A whistle is blown at the end of each trick, signalling that it is time for a reward.

Dolphin shows are certainly very popular – and trainers argue that, as well as giving the animals 'something interesting to do', it keeps them physically and mentally fit. Animal welfare groups, however, argue that they do little more than perpetuate the manipulative attitude we have towards nature. Some shows can be very demeaning, and onlookers inevitably leave with the 'wrong' impression.

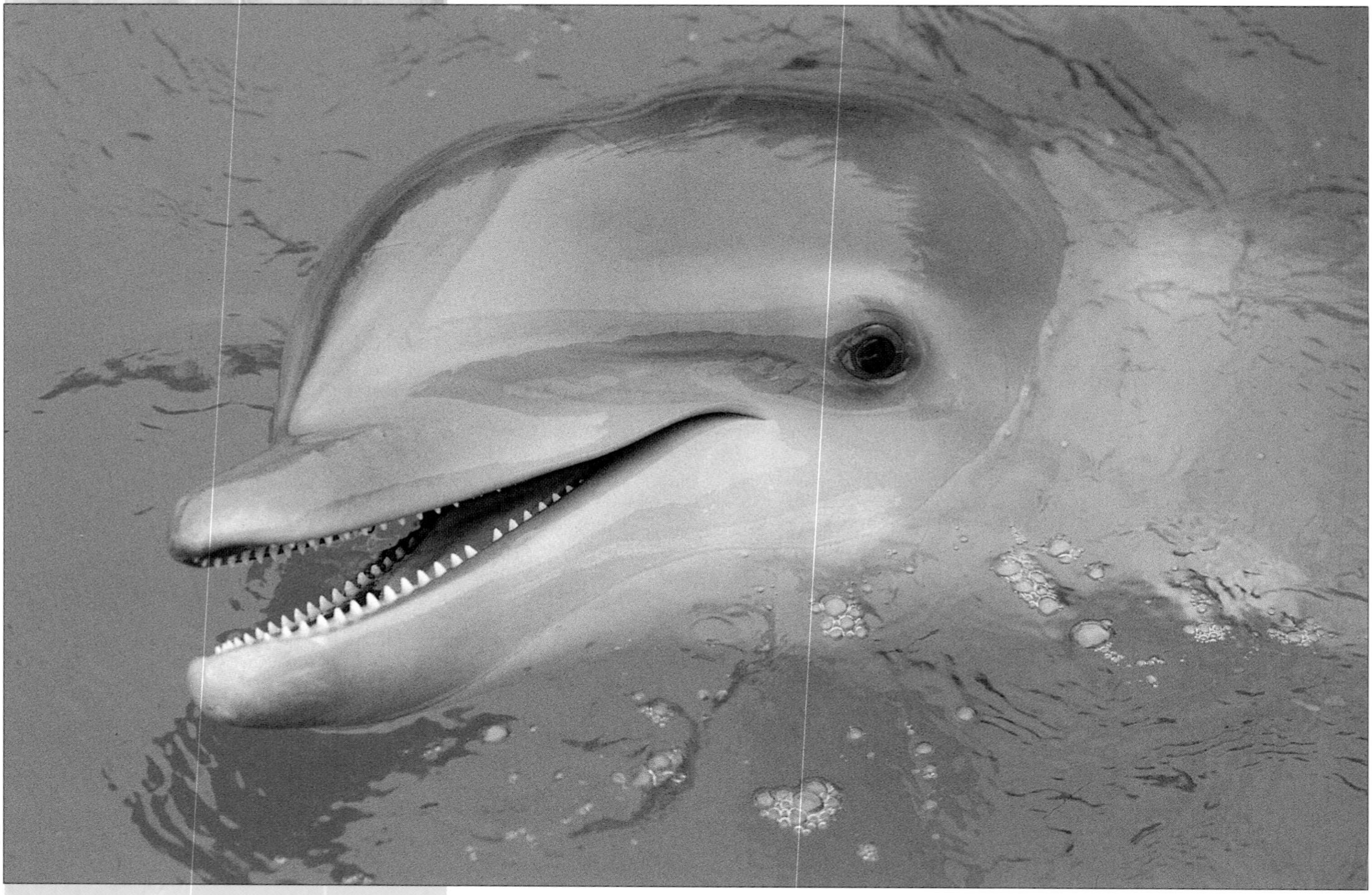

Some captive dolphins live in spacious enclosures next to the sea, and are well cared for by experienced handlers and vets, but many others are forced to live in tiny concrete tanks and receive little care and attention.

Educational and Research Opportunities Few marine parks and aquariums take full advantage of the great potential for educating and informing the public. Some are interested only in providing cheap entertainment for profit. Others give commentaries that are so carefully worded (to avoid criticism from people concerned about keeping dolphins in captivity) that they have become grossly inaccurate. In fact, it is hard to believe that some commentaries have not been prepared intentionally to mislead. There are exceptions, of course, and the best facilities provide both comprehensive and accurate information, ensuring that people leave enlightened and fairly well-informed.

However, it could be argued that watching captive dolphins jumping through hoops or swimming around in tanks is not essential to the learning process. It certainly bears little resemblance to encountering them in the wild, and may give out confusing messages. After all, people can learn about dolphins without needing to see them in real life; it is rather like learning about the Moon without actually standing on it. But many protagonists argue that a captive dolphin offers the only chance most people will have to experience the animal in real life – and that this makes all the difference.

The question is simply this: 'Would there be less support for dolphin conservation if there were no dolphins in captivity?' A real living animal is more likely to trigger the emotions than words, photographs or films, but these could be a strong 'second best'. In years to come, it may even be possible to use computer technology to simulate virtual-reality encounters with dolphins, so perhaps this could be an acceptable compromise. Unfortunately, it will probably never be possible to give an objective answer.

A less-well-publicized argument for keeping dolphins in captivity is research. It can be difficult, or even impossible, to study dolphins at close range and for extended periods in the wild, but in captivity they can be observed around the clock. Knowing their sex, age, reproductive status and dominance enables researchers to learn a great deal about their individual and social behaviour. Being able to control conditions in captivity has allowed experiments on everything from the physiology of diving to sleeping and resting. A great deal has already been learnt by studying dolphins in captivity – and it is often argued that some of this knowledge may one day help to save dolphins in the wild.

Research on captive dolphins is not without its critics. Captivity obviously affects behaviour in many ways and – even in large enclosures – the dolphins are unable to carry out all their normal activities. This certainly limits the possibilities for conclusive research work and, undoubtedly, many studies can only be satisfactorily carried out under more natural conditions. It is also argued that any discoveries made in captivity are so distorted that they give a thoroughly inadequate picture of the wild situation.

Ultimately, there is no 'right' or 'wrong' answer to the captivity question – certainly no simple one. It is a complex issue involving a bewildering range of establishments, from badly run zoos with poorly treated dolphins in tiny concrete tanks to professional marine parks with large enclosures and the best care that money can buy. It also involves a great many different people, including businessmen, trainers, biologists, conservation groups, animal welfare groups, and fee-paying members of the public. It is not surprising that everyone seems to have a different opinion on the subject.

Military Dolphins

Horses, elephants, dogs and other animals have been used in war since time immemorial. They have been put into service as beasts of burden, for sniffing out explosives and for a variety of other activities. But the use of dolphins is particularly insidious and sinister, since they are trained to accomplish tasks that are considered too risky and dangerous for people. If numerous reports are correct, they have become the living weapons of war.

Dolphins have been used for military purposes since the late 1950s. The American and Russian navies have both been involved and, since much of the information on this controversial subject is highly secret, it is possible that their use by other navies may have gone unrecorded.

The limited information available refers mainly to the U.S. Navy. It is believed that the original aim was to study dolphin sonar, sensory systems and diving physiology, in order to develop more sophisticated naval equipment. There were plans to model more hydrodynamic nuclear submarines and torpedoes on the dolphin body shape and to develop more advanced dolphin-like sonar. But this expanded rapidly into other fields of research, aimed specifically at using dolphins instead of human divers for particularly difficult tasks. There is a well-known example of a bottlenose dolphin, called Tuffy, who was deployed in a project at Sealab II in La Jolla, California. Tuffy was trained to carry tools and messages between the underwater laboratory and the surface, and was able to undertake a variety of other tasks that were physically impossible for human divers.

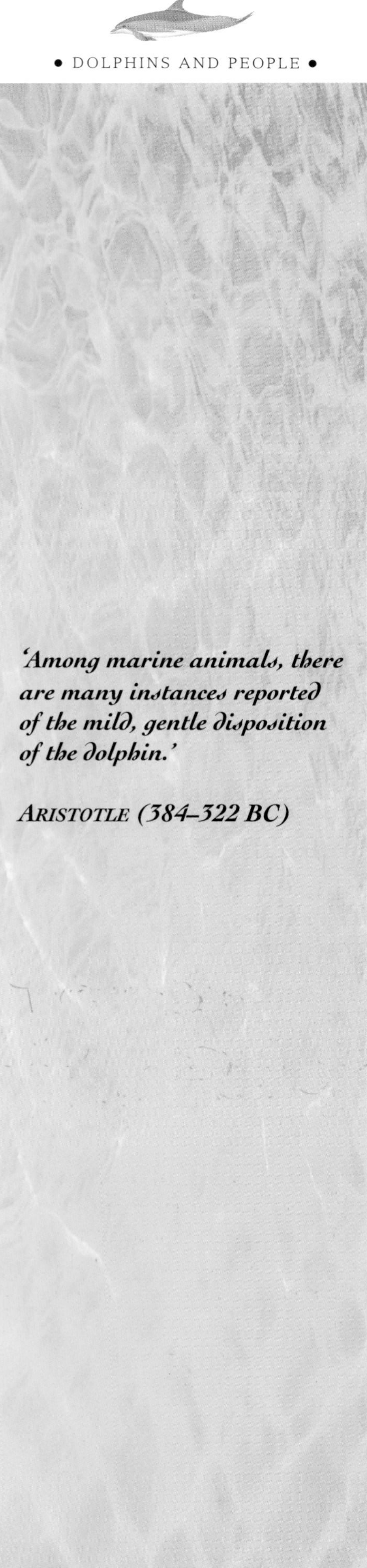

'Among marine animals, there are many instances reported of the mild, gentle disposition of the dolphin.'

ARISTOTLE (384–322 BC)

It was then decided to use dolphins as 'unmanned submarines' and 'special agents' – and there was soon a hidden agenda of secret research and training. A special programme was reputedly started to train dolphins to attack enemy frogmen and, worst of all, to act as unwitting 'kamikaze divers' for search-and-destroy missions against enemy mines and vessels.

The U.S. Navy began its controversial Marine Mammal Programme in 1959, with one bottlenose dolphin. By 1994, the programme had grown to 101 bottlenose dolphins, as well as a further twenty-two sea lions and assorted whales, costing an estimated $3.5 million in maintenance alone. Until a few years ago, the animals were kept at naval bases in Hawaii, Key West and San Diego, but recent cutbacks following the collapse of the Soviet Union have forced the training facilities in Hawaii and Florida to close. The entire programme has been absorbed by the San Diego operation.

Many dolphins and other marine mammals have died during the life of the programme, amid claims by naval employees that they are cruelly treated. There are still reports of food deprivation, solitary confinement, the use of muzzles and even corporal punishment being used in the military training process. But the Navy denies such claims, and says that 'most' of the dolphins are even 'exercised' in the open sea three to five times a week.

It is believed that approximately half the dolphins are used in research on their sonar systems and deep-diving capabilities. The rest are being trained for more controversial tasks.

The U.S. Navy has always denied training dolphins to carry mines to enemy ships, claiming that it would be a waste of both time and money, since dolphins are expensive to buy and train. It also denies training them as attack animals in a 'swimmer nullification' programme. However, there is evidence that dolphins have been used in the field on at least two occasions.

Critics of the use of dolphins for military purposes point out that dolphins are independent and unpredictable animals, and too obstreperous to be relied on 100 per cent of the time. Apart from anything else, they quickly lose interest in tedious tasks, and are apt to wander 'off-duty'.

In December 1970, six bottlenose dolphins were sent on a Vietnam War mission. Kept in nets suspended from pontoons, their job was to protect a naval base at Cam Ranh Bay from enemy frogmen. In 1976, a key member of the Navy dolphin project told a Senate Committee that the dolphins were 'armed' with large hypodermic needles strapped to their beaks; these were fitted with carbon dioxide cartridges that were designed to explode when injected into hostile divers. The dolphins had been trained to hunt out any humans swimming in the water and then to prod them with their beaks – thereby, in all innocence, giving a massive and fatal injection of gas. Again, however, the U.S. Navy denies these claims, and indeed there is no record of intruders being detected during the operation.

The second occasion involved six bottlenose dolphins that were used to protect U.S. Navy ships in the Persian Gulf. Their role was mainly underwater surveillance, in particular to detect Iranian anti-shipping mines and to protect the Navy's floating command post from attack by underwater saboteurs. But they only lasted for eight months (1987–88) and had to be returned to the States when the water temperatures rose too high.

Bottlenose dolphins have been trained by navies for a wide range of tasks, from helping divers in trouble to 'swimmer nullification' programmes, which involve injecting enemy frogmen with explosive carbon dioxide cartridges.

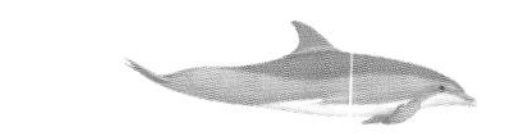

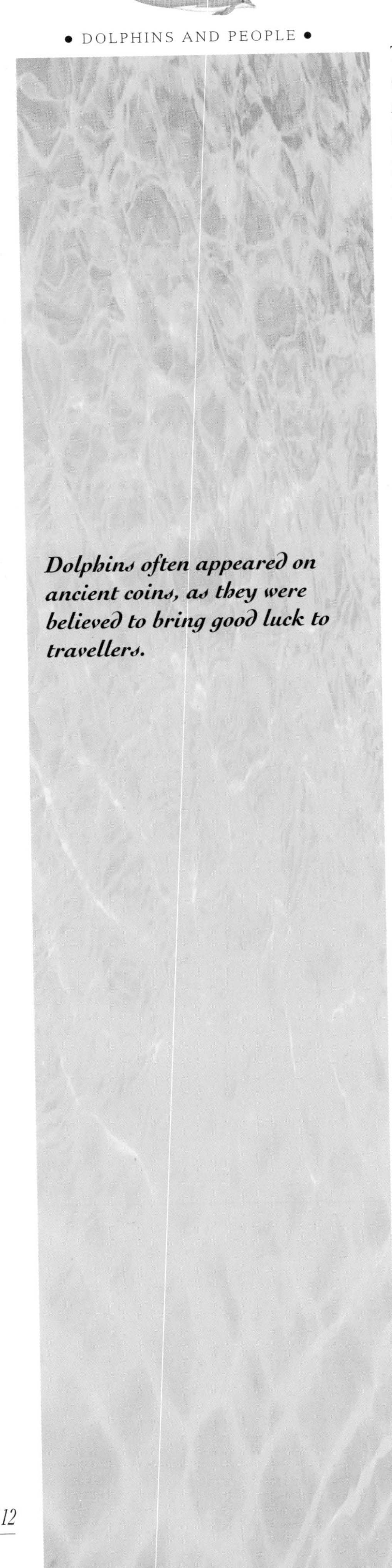

Dolphins often appeared on ancient coins, as they were believed to bring good luck to travellers.

There could have been a third occasion, if it were not for the determined efforts of a coalition of animal welfare groups in the States. In 1990, they won a case to prevent deployment of sixteen dolphins at the Bangor Naval Submarine Base, in Puget Sound, Washington State. They were to be used as 'guard dolphins' to protect a fleet of Trident nuclear submarines. When the plan became public knowledge, it caused a huge outcry in America, especially since the dolphins were going to be transported from their warm natural home in the Gulf of Mexico to the cold waters of Washington State. It is almost certain that this move would have doomed them to perish.

In addition to ethical considerations, if the use of dolphins in this way is allowed to escalate, there are several major concerns. Firstly, in a hostile situation, if both sides of a conflict are using dolphins for military purposes, all dolphins in a battle zone would have to be treated as potential enemies. Who is to know which side they are on? Therefore, there would be a real temptation to poison the surrounding waters in order to remove the threat. This may seem a little far-fetched, but already it is claimed that the U.S. Navy is investigating devices which can jam the sonar of 'enemy dolphins'.

Another potential problem concerns military dolphins that have escaped from captivity. The U.S. Navy has already admitted that some of its animals are roaming free. Its trainers work regularly with dolphins untethered in the open sea and, apparently, after more than 200,000 outings, dolphins have failed to return on nine occasions. This may be a small proportion, but no-one knows what these escapees might do if they encounter an innocent recreational diver or swimmer.

Many experts are also concerned about the feasibility of using dolphins in any defence/offence programme. They believe that, from the military point of view, it is all a waste of effort. Dolphins are independent and unpredictable animals, and too obstreperous to be relied on 100 per cent of the time. Apart from anything else, they quickly lose interest in tedious tasks, and are apt to wander off-duty. As one retired dolphin trainer put it, 'I wouldn't feel at all safe with a bunch of bored and mischievous dolphins protecting a fleet of our Trident nuclear submarines'.

In the spring of 1994, the U.S. Navy announced that it wanted to give away as many as thirty bottlenose dolphins to marine parks and aquariums. The news was heralded by many animal welfare groups as the death cry of its programme, but such a suggestion has been denied by the Navy itself. It has always claimed that the dolphins were simply 'excess to requirements', and pledged to continue caring for any animals for which they could not find a new home.

The last word should perhaps be left to dolphin experts Michael Donoghue and Anne Wheeler. They make a thought-provoking observation in their excellent book *Dolphins: Their Life and Survival*: 'The idea of using creatures which have become such symbols of peace and harmony to help humans kill each other is a final stroke of black irony.'

Will We Ever be Able to Talk to Dolphins?

The possibility that one day we may be able to talk to dolphins has captured the human imagination for centuries. When scientists first started to eavesdrop on their incessant underwater chattering, they heard a medley of whistles, barks, grunts, squeaks and squawks that sounded remarkably like some kind of language. It seemed that all we had to do was to work out what they were saying. Some people predicted that we would be conversing with dolphins within a few decades; others went so far as to suggest that if an alien intelligence were to attempt to communicate with life on earth, it might choose dolphins in preference to humans. But these are dreams that have yet to come true.

We are still a long way from understanding how dolphins communicate with one another, and stories about breakthroughs in this field have often been greatly exaggerated by the media. In fact, it is even unclear whether they have a true spoken language of their own – let alone, whether we will ever be able to speak it ourselves.

There is no doubt that dolphins communicate. At the very least, using a combination of sound and body language, they can pass on information about everything from their identity (each dolphin is believed to have its own unique 'signature whistle') to their emotional state. In fact, judging by the variety of sounds and body postures they make, it is quite possible that they pass a wealth of information from one individual to another. But a series of simple commands and signals does not necessarily constitute a real language. The big

Stories about breakthroughs in dolphin communication have often been exaggerated by the media, and whether or not we will ever be able to find a common language with dolphins is still open to conjecture.

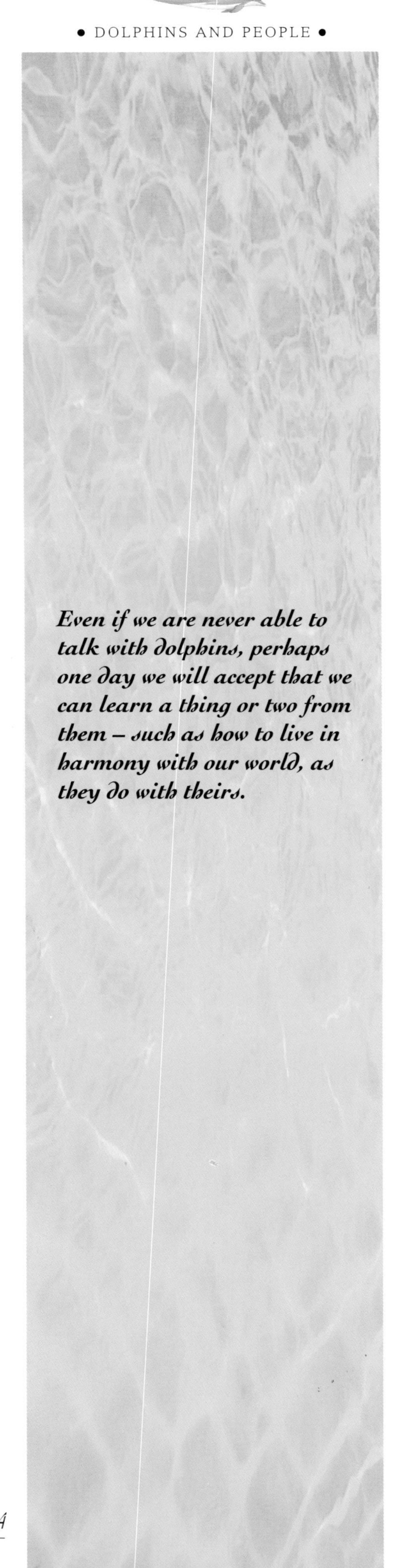

Even if we are never able to talk with dolphins, perhaps one day we will accept that we can learn a thing or two from them – such as how to live in harmony with our world, as they do with theirs.

question is whether they understand what they are saying – in other words, can they discuss more abstract concepts, such as changes in the weather or their plans for the future?

Dolphin Language Studies There have been relatively few studies on dolphin language in the wild. One of the best known has been carried out on a population of Atlantic spotted dolphins in The Bahamas since 1985. Using video recordings and computer analyses of dolphin sounds, biologist Denise Herzing has built up a picture of how the dolphins use particular sounds and body language to communicate. She has identified a fascinating range of signals, including a 'Mum!' emitted by young calves when they are separated from their mothers; a 'Keep together' emitted by different members of a school; and a 'Help!' emitted by injured or unwell dolphins. Although this alone does not constitute a language, it could be interpreted as a very simple vocabulary.

Much of the research in this field has focused on teaching dolphins to learn a human language, rather than trying to understand theirs. Similar work with captive gorillas has been enormously successful, using sign language to develop a basic form of two-way communication. A female gorilla named Koko not only mastered basic English, but also demonstrated many human attributes such as joking, lying, teasing and insulting. Unfortunately, it is impossible to use the same technique with captive dolphins, simply because they are unable to use sign language themselves. But the fact that they are skilled mimics and quick learners, and have excellent memories, can be used in other ways.

A remarkable study with captive bottlenose dolphins at the University of Hawaii involved generating 'words' of a language as sounds made by computer. These were broadcast underwater. (Similar studies have used hand and arm signals instead, with equally interesting results). Initially, the dolphins were taught single words such as 'fetch', 'ball' and 'hoop' but, gradually, they were taught to understand two words strung together in simple sentences. From a total of 600 two-word sentence instructions, they gave correct responses about 80 per cent of the time, and were eventually taught to respond to sentences up to five words long. They were even able to communicate details of their surroundings, such as whether a ball was in the tank or not. More importantly, they could take account of both the meaning and grammatical arrangement of the words. They could distinguish, for example, between 'ball-fetch-hoop' (which means 'get the ball and take it to the hoop') and 'hoop-fetch-ball' (which means the opposite – 'get the hoop and take it to the ball').

This kind of research proves nothing about dolphin communication in the wild, and does not prove that dolphins have their own language, but it does demonstrate that they can grasp the essential elements of any human language. In other words, they seem to have the potential to develop a language, even if they have not done so independently. For many people, the most exciting discovery is that some form of inter-species communication can exist. But whether this is of a level more akin to communicating with a dog, or whether it is closer to chatting with a human friend, is a subject of continuing controversy.

Another interesting experiment involved two dolphins in separate tanks, visually screened from one another but able to communicate by sound. The male dolphin's tank was supplied with two levers, and he was given a food reward every time he pressed the correct one. The female's tank was supplied with two lights. The left light in the female's tank was illuminated if the left lever in the male's tank was the correct one to release food, and vice versa. The male pressed the correct lever every time, almost without fail, using information supplied by the female.

No-one can be sure where all this research will lead, of course. A major stumbling block has been that dolphins often 'speak' in frequencies well beyond the range of human hearing, although computers are going some way to rectify this problem. It has even been suggested that dolphins are telepathic, and may be able to communicate without speech; many trainers report telepathic experiences with them. If this is true, it would open up a whole new range of possibilities – and might even help to explain why dolphins have such a profound effect on so many people. It is also possible that some species and populations have evolved a vocalized language, while others have not. However, such theories are pure conjecture and, in reality, we are still a very long way from understanding what really goes on inside the dolphin's mind.

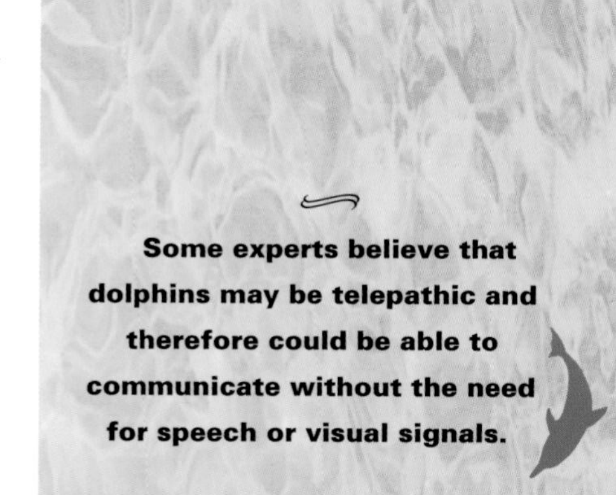

Some experts believe that
dolphins may be telepathic and
therefore could be able to
communicate without the need
for speech or visual signals.

The Healing Power of Dolphins

Research in several countries suggests that dolphins may be able to trigger the healing process in people. It is a claim that has had more than its fair share of sceptics, and it is especially difficult to demonstrate scientifically. However, there are so many accounts of dolphins alleviating cases of chronic depression or anxiety, enhancing recovery from life-threatening illnesses such as cancer, and even speeding up the learning potential of handicapped children, that biologists and doctors around the world are beginning to take it seriously.

Consider some of the evidence. One American study involved two groups of autistic children who were believed to be 'beyond hope'. One group was allowed to play with plastic dolphins on a beach, while the other was taken

into the water to swim with some real dolphins. The beach children showed no improvement in their condition, but the water children improved dramatically soon afterwards. Other American studies have demonstrated that dolphins can help handicapped children to learn four times more quickly than is possible with other teaching methods, and to retain the information for a longer period of time. No-one knows exactly how or why, but 'dolphin therapy' is believed to give them more confidence in their own abilities. It is gaining so much respect in the U.S. that some doctors refer handicapped children to dolphin therapy centres, and several health insurance companies will even cover the cost.

Many people suffering from anxiety and depression also seem to benefit from the experience of swimming with dolphins. There is no concrete scientific proof that jumping in the water with them has any long-term benefit, but there are some spectacular examples that provide plenty of intriguing circumstantial evidence.

Horace Dobbs, a world-renowned expert on the healing power of dolphins, tells the story of a man who was being treated for chronic depression and had not been able to work for twelve years. Despite the help of specialists, chemotherapy, counselling and periods in psychiatric wards, his condition did

not improve. In his own words, he was living in 'a black pit of despair'. Then in 1985 Dobbs took the man to swim with Simo, a friendly bottlenose dolphin living near the tiny fishing village of Solva, in Wales. Within moments, the two became inseparable. The man broke his silence and spoke to Simo as if he were talking to an old friend. By the time he had clambered back into the boat, his wife could see traces of the man she had known and loved, and she broke down and cried. For the first time in all those years, the black cloud had started to lift.

There is little doubt that a dolphin can have a powerful effect on human emotions. Few people remain unmoved by a close encounter, especially if they are in the water meeting the dolphin on its own terms. It is an experience that affects everyone in their own way; many report feeling euphoric or uplifted, others burst into tears and feel overwhelmed. But either way, it seems to elicit an extreme response.

This is particularly interesting because emotions and health of mind play very important roles in the healing process. Good health is more than a mere absence of disease. Contentment, peace of mind, flowing energy and a deep sense of security are all essential ingredients of total well-being.

Few people would deny that dolphins have an uplifting effect on the human spirit; these children will never forget their close encounter with a small school of common dolphins off the coast of Gibraltar.

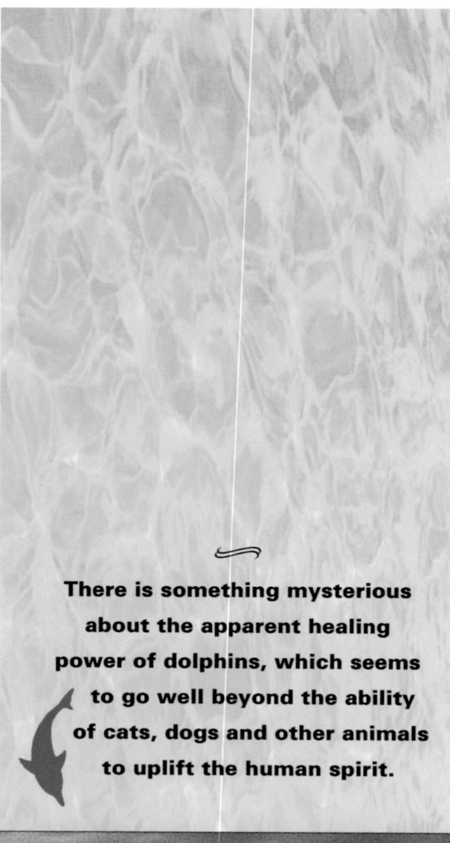

There is something mysterious about the apparent healing power of dolphins, which seems to go well beyond the ability of cats, dogs and other animals to uplift the human spirit.

It has been known for many years that dogs, cats and other animals can play a vital role in maintaining a healthy mind, and a healthy body by association. They help anxious people to relax, at least partly because their affection is unconditional – it bears no relation to sex, age, size, colour, shape or appearance. Whether dolphin therapy works on exactly the same basis, or whether dolphins have an extra-special quality that we have yet to identify, no-one really knows.

It is possible that having to overcome a fear of swimming with such a large and powerful animal may give the dolphin an edge over cats and dogs. But many people believe that there is much more to dolphin therapy than that and, while all their theories are purely speculative, they are nonetheless intriguing. One focuses on the ultrasonic sounds that dolphins produce: they may work as a kind of natural radiation therapy, for example stimulating the release of endorphins (natural painkillers). Another focuses on the energy fields that are believed to surround the body. Some people, who are inwardly happy, have a particular aura or presence that creates a positive feeling in other people. Perhaps dolphins have a similar, more powerful aura? Or perhaps they are even able to diagnose and re-adjust our energy fields?

Intriguingly, dolphins seem able to recognize depression or illness in people. Researchers have found, time and again, that dolphins have an uncanny ability to home in on the people who most need help, even when there are other people in the water. Again, no-one can explain how they are able to do this. One possibility is that, if they are highly sensitive to energy fields, they may be able to pick up

subtle abnormalities in the fields of people with health problems. Another is that they can pick up problems with their sophisticated sonar, which may enable them to 'see' inside the human body. It may even be psychological: it is often suggested that dolphins are telepathic (they certainly seem to be more intuitive than most people), and so they may be able to read minds and emotions.

There are so many unanswered questions (not least of which is a moral one: can we justify this form of dolphin exploitation, as it is seen by some people, for human benefit?). We do not even know if the 'dolphin effect' is physical, emotional or spiritual. But even if it is entirely in our own minds – and there is nothing unique about the dolphins themselves – it may yet prove to be a valuable alternative to more conventional treatments. The lack of harmful side-effects, for instance, is an obvious advantage. And by continuing with this research – even by investigating the most unlikely lines of enquiry – we are learning more about dolphins all the time.

It has long been claimed that dolphins are able to trigger the healing process in people – and there is mounting evidence to suggest that this could well be true.

CHAPTER

8

Dolphin Watching

A close encounter with a dolphin in the wild is a thrilling and memorable experience. Who could remain untouched by the spectacular acrobatics of a long-snouted spinner dolphin as it hurls itself into the air and spins? Or the sight of 1,000 common dolphins in tight formation, making their way purposefully across the sea? Or the drama of a white-beaked dolphin riding the bow-waves of a boat, just a few feet away? These are the kind of experiences that stay with people for the rest of their lives.

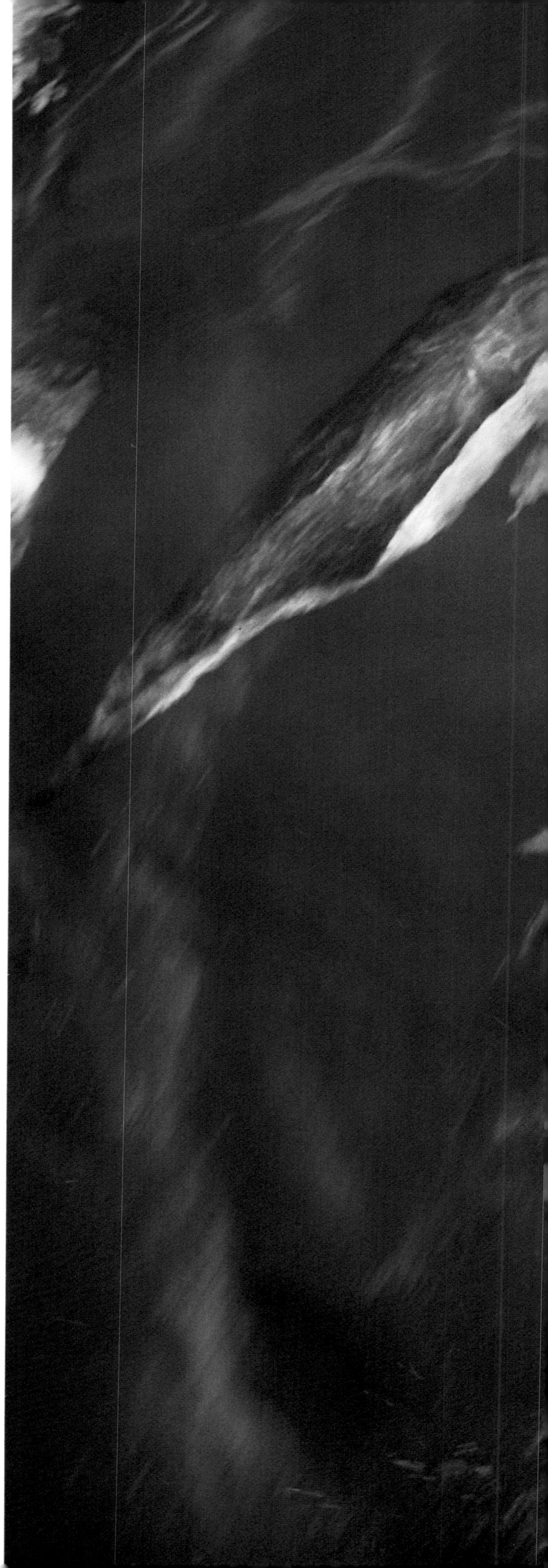

Common dolphins, Gibraltar.

The Growth in Dolphin Watching

Dolphin watching is a rapidly growing business. There are commercial operators in dozens of different countries and in almost every corner of the globe, attracting millions of people every year. Yet it is quite a new phenomenon and, not many years ago, was virtually unknown outside a few key hot spots. There was a tendency for people to go whale watching, and if they saw dolphins at the same time it was a bonus. But nowadays the dolphins themselves are getting a fair share of the attention. In Scotland's Moray Firth, for example, where there is a resident population of about 130 bottlenose dolphins, boats offering trips to watch them have risen from one in 1990 to as many as twelve in 1995. This reflects a global trend.

Dolphin watching is now of considerable economic and educational importance. It can provide an important source of revenue for local communities, as well as providing an ideal opportunity to interest and educate people in wider marine issues.

But the risk is that all these human admirers will love the dolphins to death. It is sometimes easy to forget that we are uninvited guests in their world, and that we are privileged to see them. We have a responsibility to help them benefit from dolphin watching through education, fund-raising, research and a variety of other closely related activities. More importantly, we have a responsibility to cause as little disturbance as possible; dolphin watching should be an eyes-on-hands-off activity, with proper respect and etiquette the most important tools of the trade. The solution is straightforward: everyone should 'watch how they watch'.

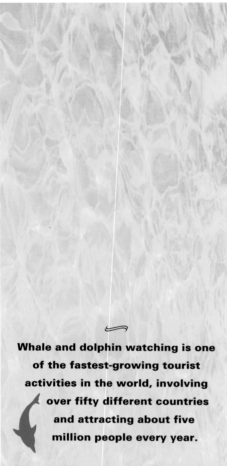

Whale and dolphin watching is one of the fastest-growing tourist activities in the world, involving over fifty different countries and attracting about five million people every year.

Where to See Dolphins

In theory, it is possible to see dolphins almost anywhere in the world where there is a coastline. A walk along the shore, a short ferry crossing, or even a harbour cruise – with luck, all of these can provide opportunities for some excellent sightings. However, it is more common for dolphins to be plentiful only in particular areas and, even then, they may be present only at certain times of the year. Therefore, without forward planning it is possible to spend

fruitless hours simply staring at an empty sea; the secret is to do a little homework beforehand.

From a boat, or the shore, the ocean can look much the same anywhere in the world. It can be either rough or calm, of course, and may change colour from one place to another, but these differences frequently seem so slight that it is not always obvious why dolphins choose to live in some areas and not in others. In fact, beneath the featureless surface, their underwater world is as varied as our own. The ocean floor has as many different physical features as dry land – towering mountain ranges, vast canyons and valleys, rugged outcrops and sweeping plains. Even the water itself has a wide range of temperatures and salinity, receives different amounts of light, has different depths, and is warmed or cooled by a variety of different currents.

Just as cheetahs live on open plains rather than jungles, and snow leopards live in mountains rather than wetlands, most dolphins are adapted to specific marine habitats. A good example is Hector's dolphin, which lives exclusively in the cool, coastal waters of New Zealand; even then, it is absent from some areas within this limited range. On the other hand, some dolphins are highly adaptable, and can be found in a wide range of habitats worldwide. The pantropical spotted dolphin, for example, is equally at home far out to sea or close to shore, and Risso's dolphin is found anywhere from cold temperate waters to warm tropical waters.

In many parts of the world it is possible to see dolphins regularly from the shore. In others, it is necessary to head out to sea for several hours, or even several days, for a better chance of finding them. Places with well-known dolphin-watching opportunities include Scotland, Wales, Ireland, Iceland, Gibraltar, Florida, The Bahamas, St. Vincent, Brazil, Australia, New Zealand and Japan – although there are a great many others, and the choice is growing all the time.

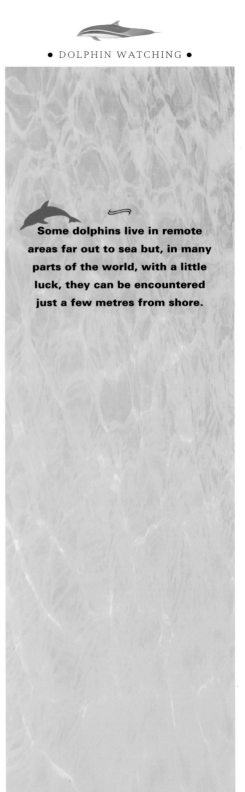

Some dolphins live in remote areas far out to sea but, in many parts of the world, with a little luck, they can be encountered just a few metres from shore.

How to Watch Dolphins

There are many ways to watch dolphins in the wild – from the shore; from the air; underwater; and from a host of different vessels including yachts, motor cruisers, rubber inflatables, research boats, kayaks, and even huge ocean-going ships. But there are really just two golden rules to successful dolphin watching: the first, and most important, is to cause as little disturbance as possible; the second is to be patient.

Joining a properly organized trip is probably the best way to see dolphins. Most commercial trips have a high success rate in spotting dolphins, because they tend to concentrate on well-known populations and operate during the appropriate seasons. The better ones also have expert naturalist-guides who are not only experienced at finding dolphins but can also interpret interesting behavioural activities and are able to provide a wealth of background information. More importantly, the skippers know (or should know) how to manoeuvre the boat around dolphins safely. Without due care and attention, the noise and movement of boats can be unnecessarily stressful, and there is always the risk of propellers causing serious injury.

It is difficult to measure the disturbance caused by dolphin watching. In some areas, the animals are fairly accustomed to swimming around a motley collection of vessels without injuring themselves on the propellers, while in other areas accidents are more common. But simply disturbing or scattering a group may separate mothers and calves, for example, and thereby increase their vulnerability. There is little doubt that heavy pressure over prolonged periods can have a negative impact.

Equipment Several items of equipment can be extremely useful for dolphin watching (although in some parts of the world just a pair of eyes will suffice). Binoculars are handy for spotting dolphins at a distance, identifying different species and observing behaviour in more detail. There is always a temptation to buy the pair with the highest magnification, but anything more than 10x can make it almost impossible to hold them steady on a boat, especially in choppy seas. Professional researchers tend to use binoculars with 7x or 8x magnification.

Many people like to take a camera, and some outstanding pictures have been taken of dolphins over the years, even with the simplest of equipment. However, a good 35mm SLR camera is ideal. Motordrives are invaluable; since dolphins are always on the move, most professional photographers take lots of pictures every time something interesting happens, in the hope of getting one or two really good shots on a roll. Long lenses tend to be difficult to hold steady on boats, at least in any but the calmest of seas, and changing lenses can be a problem if there is a lot of saltwater spray. The ideal solution is a zoom lens of around 80–200mm, which will cope with most eventualities. The key to successful video photography is rather similar: take lots of film and, when there are dolphins around, keep the camera running as you attempt to follow them underwater. Eventually, they will surface or breach in exactly the right place.

It is also worth carrying a notebook and pen. Keeping detailed notes is an excellent way of building up a good basic knowledge for identification purposes and for interpreting different behaviour patterns. Also take suntan lotion, seasickness tablets and Polaroid sunglasses (which not only reduce the sun's glare, but are also excellent for following the dolphins underwater). Life jackets are usually provided on organized trips, if necessary. Many boat operators also have a hydrophone on board, which adds a whole new dimension to the dolphin-watching experience. Finally, since dolphin watching often involves getting wet, take waterproof clothes, rubber-soled shoes in case of a wet deck and a waterproof bag to protect your equipment.

Many dolphin species tend to be plentiful only in particular areas and, even then, may be present only at certain times of the year; a little research and forward planning can increase the chance of sightings and close encounters immeasurably. The best place to see these Atlantic spotted dolphins is on Little Bahama Bank, in The Bahamas.

Dolphin watching often involves getting wet, so take waterproof clothes, rubber-soled deck shoes, and a waterproof bag to protect your equipment. Binoculars are invaluable for spotting dolphins in the distance, as well as for studying their behaviour and identifying different species.

Dolphin-watching Etiquette

There are no standard guidelines for dolphin watching and even expert opinion differs on the best approach. The main problem is the number of variables. Watching dolphins at rest requires a different technique to watching them bow-riding or feeding, for example, and their level of tolerance towards a kayak is likely to be different to their tolerance towards a rigid-hulled inflatable or yacht. It all depends on the species, the local conditions, the overall level of disturbance in the area, the behaviour of the animals, the type of boat being used and a range of other factors.

In some parts of the world, there are strict regulations for dolphin watching, and it is important to be familiar with these before heading out to sea. Nevertheless, boat handling around dolphins can be especially tricky for people with little experience, who may find it difficult to interpret their behaviour or anticipate their movements. As dolphins rarely stay still, it can be difficult to put guideline theories into practice – even with the best of intentions.

The simple dos and don'ts opposite are not foolproof, but they are designed to help with some of the key points to bear in mind when manoeuvring a boat around dolphins. The golden rule is simple: if in any doubt, slow down and keep your distance.

It should go without saying not to throw rubbish into the sea, although it is surprising how often some dolphin watchers toss their crisp and cigarette packets, polystyrene cups, sweet wrappers and other rubbish over the side. Similarly, boat operators should refrain from disposing of fuel, oil or other contaminants, except in appropriate containers on shore.

Finally, if you see anyone mistreating or behaving irresponsibly around dolphins, report them to the proper authorities or to an appropriate conservation group as soon as possible.

The best dolphin-watching trips have experienced naturalists on board, who are skilled at finding the animals and provide interesting and informative commentaries, as well as skippers who are well-versed in dolphin-watching etiquette.

There are really just two golden rules for successful dolphin watching: the first and most important is to cause as little disturbance as possible, the second is to be patient. These Japanese dolphin watchers spent most of the day staring at an empty sea, but were eventually rewarded with a spectacular close encounter with a Risso's dolphin.

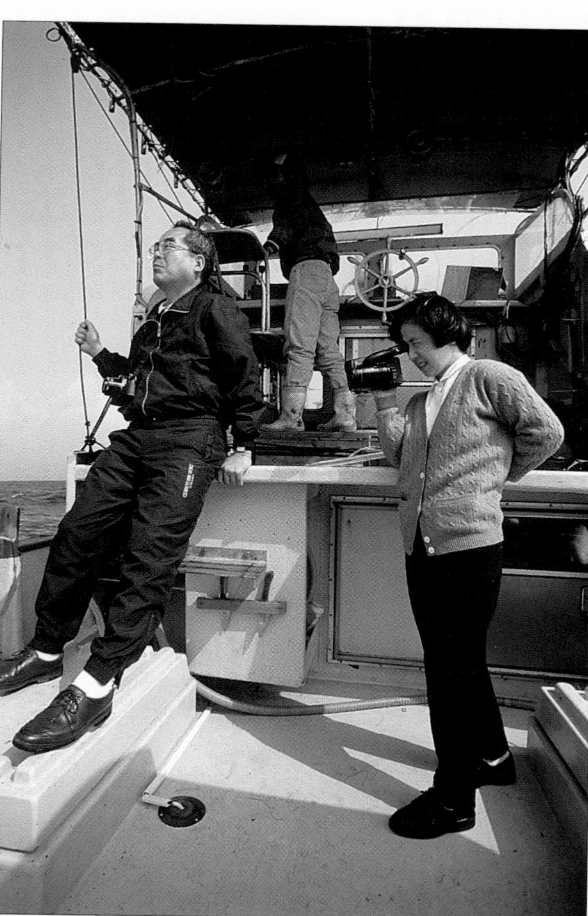

This bottlenose dolphin had a close encounter with a boat propeller and was critically ill for months; fortunately, its wounds eventually healed and it survived.

DOLPHIN WATCHING DOS AND DON'TS

- Dolphins are frequently curious, so whenever possible let them approach you.
- When the dolphins are feeding or are obviously preoccupied, and seem uninterested in the boat, do not approach too closely (observe them quietly, from a sensible distance).
- When approaching a group of dolphins, come in from a position parallel and slightly to the rear - not from the front or immediately behind.
- Do not try and get the boat in the middle of a large school of dolphins. It is better to watch from one side.
- Always approach and depart slowly (never faster than an idle or 'no wake' speed).
- Avoid sudden changes in speed or direction.
- Keep noise levels to a minimum (no horns, whistles, or revving motors).
- Never chase or harass dolphins, and try not to separate or scatter groups.
- When stationary, especially if there are dolphins near the propeller, keep the engine in neutral (alternatively, if you are travelling and the dolphins are wake-riding, do not make sudden bursts of speed or changes in direction).
- If the dolphins are bow-riding, do not stop or slow down suddenly (this can confuse and alarm them as much as sudden acceleration).
- Limit the time spent with any group of dolphins to 15–30 minutes (but if they appear to be disturbed by your presence, leave much sooner).
- Avoid overcrowding (one boat is a lot less threatening than three or four).
- Do not attempt to feed the dolphins.

Swimming with Dolphins

Swimming with dolphins is such an overwhelming experience that it is impossible to describe in mere words. In fact, it is so awe-inspiring and thrilling that it changes many people's lives. Hundreds of thousands of people around the world have been lucky enough to swim with wild dolphins over the years – with Atlantic spotted dolphins in The Bahamas, friendly bottlenose dolphins anywhere from Ireland to Florida, dusky dolphins in New Zealand, and many more.

In many cases, it is a harmless and educational activity. After all, there is no way we can impose our company on the dolphins - if they are not interested, they can just swim away. However, some experts question the wisdom of swimming with dolphins. Firstly, there is a possible risk to the dolphins themselves – people could pass on human diseases (for which the dolphins may have no natural immunity), and the human/dolphin interactions may encourage abnormal behaviour. Secondly, there is a potential risk to the people – dolphins can be dangerous if the swimmers are insensitive to their moods and actions; they are wild animals and can therefore behave unpredictably. They also have much rougher ways of relating to each other than most people are used to, and accidents occasionally happen.

The trouble is that each dolphin encounter is different. In some cases, remaining passive in the water can provoke surprisingly aggressive behaviour; or it may provoke overt 'sexual' contact. In other cases, the dolphins simply get bored and swim away. Even the friendliest dolphins are not immune to mood swings. If provoked, they sometimes defend themselves with a hard tail slap, a bite, an aggressive shove, or even a head-butt. In the early 1980s, for example, a large male bottlenose dolphin named Percy made friends with human

This wild bottlenose dolphin, called Maui, arrived in Kaikoura, New Zealand, in August 1992 – and soon became a popular member of the local community. Maui is seen here with her best friend, Carol, who swam with her every evening after work.

Guidelines for Swimming with Dolphins

Unfortunately, there are no set guidelines for swimming with dolphins that can be applied to all animals and all situations. The requirements vary from species to species, individual to individual and place to place. They are also dependent on whether people are swimming with a single dolphin or a large school, and on whether or not the animals are used to people in the water.

These particular guidelines, which are really just common sense, have been designed as a basic starting point. They should be adapted to suit local conditions.

1. PERSONAL SAFETY

✳ Wear a buoyancy aid (especially if you are not a strong swimmer).

✳ Be aware of the strength and direction of local currents.

✳ Do not stray too far from the boat (or shore).

✳ Be vigilant near boats – a whirling propeller can be lethal – and make sure you can be seen by all boat users in the area.

✳ If at all possible, swim in the company of a dolphin expert.

✳ Be aware of the power and strength of the dolphin.

✳ Do not attempt to touch the dolphin unless it offers a clear invitation (reaching out may be interpreted as a threat).

✳ Do not try to hitch a ride on the dolphin's back.

✳ If the dolphin knocks or nips you, or becomes unusually boisterous, do not panic, but keep your arms by your side and exit slowly from the water.

✳ Do not lie on your back in the water (some dolphins do not like this, and can become aggressive as a result).

2. DOLPHIN SAFETY

✳ Never touch the dolphin on the blowhole or on the forehead.

✳ Do not wear or carry sharp objects, such as rings and other pieces of jewellery, that could accidentally damage the dolphin's skin and may cause infection.

✳ Do not swim if you are physically ill – you may pass on your germs to the dolphin.

3. GETTING THE MOST OUT OF THE ENCOUNTER

✳ Slip quietly into the water to avoid frightening the dolphin unnecessarily.

✳ While in the water, move around as much as possible to keep the dolphin interested (dive beneath the surface and do the loop-the-loop, for example).

✳ Move as gracefully and rhythmically as possible, with your hands crossed behind your back, mimicking the dolphin.

✳ Do not crowd or chase the dolphin.

✳ Try not to control the dolphin or what it does – let it take the initiative.

swimmers at Portreath, in Cornwall, and then suddenly became unpredictable; sometimes he was gentle, but at other times he would butt people in the chest, smash against surfboards and even carry swimmers out to sea. There are many other examples of unpredictable behaviour, where dolphins have actively prevented people from swimming ashore, or have pinned divers to the seabed.

In a tiny minority of cases, dolphins can become dangerous, and there have been accidents over the years. An extreme example occurred in Brazil, in December 1994, when one man died and another was injured after being attacked by a male bottlenose dolphin at a beach near Sao Paulo; according to onlookers, the two men had been trying to ride on its back, and may even have been attempting to push something down its blowhole.

Potential dangers such as these should serve as a reminder that dolphins, like all wild animals, have to be approached with caution and respect. Although swimming with dolphins can still be one of the most exciting wildlife experiences, it does need to be well managed, and ideally should take place under the watchful eye of an expert.

It is unusual for groups of dolphins to seek out human company, but on Little Bahama Bank, to the north of The Bahamas, Atlantic spotted dolphins frequently join human swimmers for minutes or even hours at a time.

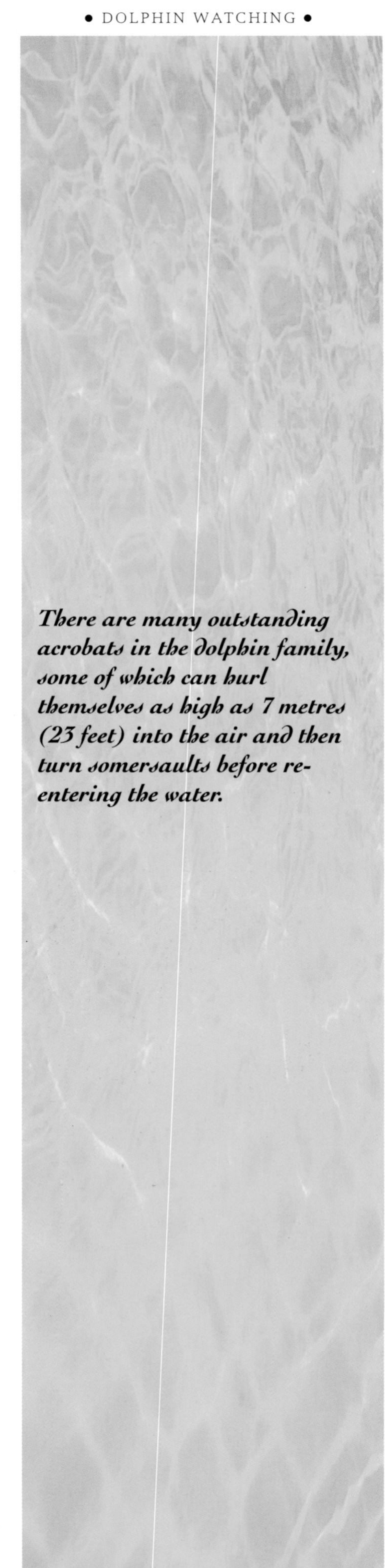

There are many outstanding acrobats in the dolphin family, some of which can hurl themselves as high as 7 metres (23 feet) into the air and then turn somersaults before re-entering the water.

Recognizing Behaviour Patterns

Surprisingly little is known about dolphin behaviour. Over the years, a wide range of activities has been observed and a number have been given official names, but in many cases their precise meanings are still something of a mystery. It is quite possible that there are different explanations for different occasions, according to the species, the age and sex of the animal, and the context in which the activity is taking place.

'Breaching' is undoubtedly the most spectacular of all surface activities. The dolphin launches itself into the air head-first and then falls back into the water with a splash. Most species have been observed breaching at one time or another. Curiously, it is not unusual for an animal to breach several times in a row and, when that happens, other dolphins frequently feel the urge to follow suit.

There are many different kinds of breach. The entire body may be propelled into the air, or only a part of the body; the dolphin may re-enter the water cleanly, with barely a splash; or it may do a belly-flop, turn on one side, or turn onto its back, and make a tremendous splash. Alternatively, it may perform a 'head-slap', which begins with a half-hearted surge and ends by pounding the head and top part of the body onto the surface. Some species can leap very high and often do complete somersaults, twists and turns before re-entering the water. The record-holder is probably the long-snouted spinner dolphin, which hurls itself up to 3 metres (9 feet 10 inches) into the air, then twists its body into sinuous curves or spins round on its longitudinal axis up to seven times in a single leap.

No-one really knows why dolphins breach. But there are numerous possible explanations: it may be a courtship display, a form of communication or signalling, a way to herd fish or dislodge parasites, a show of strength or a challenge, or perhaps it is simply for fun. Most experts believe that several (or all) of these theories are correct and that breaching has different functions in different situations.

'Lobtailing' or 'tail-slapping' describes the forceful slapping of the flukes against the water, while most of the animal is under the surface. This is more commonly seen in large whales, but dolphins sometimes slap their flukes onto the surface of the water as they dive, or when they are angry. 'Flipper-slapping' or 'pectoral slapping' is rather similar, and occurs when the dolphin rolls over at the surface and slaps one of its flippers on the water. 'Fluking' is when the dolphin lifts its tail into the air as it dives. Again, this is normally associated with large whales, but some dolphins briefly lift their tails in the same way. 'Spyhopping' is the term used to describe an interesting form of behaviour in which the dolphin pokes its head above the surface of the water, apparently to have a look around.

Swimming in the frothy wake of a boat or ship seems to be a favourite pastime of many dolphins. This is called 'wake-riding'. The dolphins surf in the waves, twist and turn or swim upside-down in the bubbles, and sometimes press their beaks right up against the stern of the vessel. They frequently ride in the bow-waves as well, jostling for the best position where they can be pushed along in the water by the force of the wave. Appropriately, this is called 'bow-riding'.

Breaching (long-snouted spinner dolphin)

Porpoising (southern rightwhale dolphin)

Lobtailing (pantropical spotted dolphin)

Spyhopping (Indo-Pacific hump-backed dolphin)

Wake-riding (hourglass dolphin)

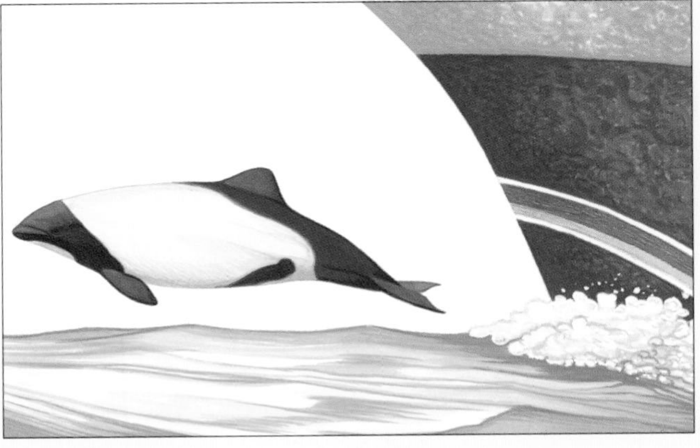

Bow-riding (Commerson's dolphin)

It is possible to see a number of interesting and easily recognizable patterns of behaviour on most dolphin-watching trips.

Problems of Identification

Identifying dolphins at sea is a special challenge. Many species look alike; one individual is rarely identical to the next; they frequently spend long periods of time underwater; and many tend to show little of themselves at the surface. Adverse sea and weather conditions, such as a heavy swell, whitecaps, high winds, driving rain, or even glaring sunshine add to the difficulties.

It is not surprising that even the world's experts are sometimes unable to identify every animal they encounter – even on official surveys, some sightings have to be logged as 'unidentified' or 'dolphin species'. However, with some background knowledge and a little practice, it is quite possible for anyone to recognize the more commonly seen and distinctive species, and eventually many of the more unusual ones as well.

The key to successful identification is a simple process of elimination. This requires a mental checklist of the main features to look for in every dolphin encountered at sea. One feature alone is rarely enough for a positive identification, so the golden rule is to gather information on as many of these features as possible before drawing any conclusions.

For dolphins, there are ten main points on this checklist: size (it is difficult to estimate length at sea, but try to compare it with something on the boat or with another object in the water); unusual features (such as the 'hump' on the backs of hump-backed dolphins); dorsal fin position, shape, and colour; body and head shape (in particular, whether the body is robust or streamlined, and if there is a prominent beak); colour and markings (bearing in mind that colours at sea appear to vary according to water clarity and light conditions); surfacing behaviour and dive sequence; breaching and other distinctive activities; the number of animals observed (bearing in mind that, at any one time, there may be many more dolphins below the surface than there are above); main habitat (coastal, open sea, riverine, etc.); and geographical location.

Identifying dolphins at sea is a challenge. Many species look alike; one individual is rarely identical to the next; they frequently spend long periods of time underwater; and many species tend to show little of themselves at the surface. This splash is being made by a bottlenose dolphin in Mexico.

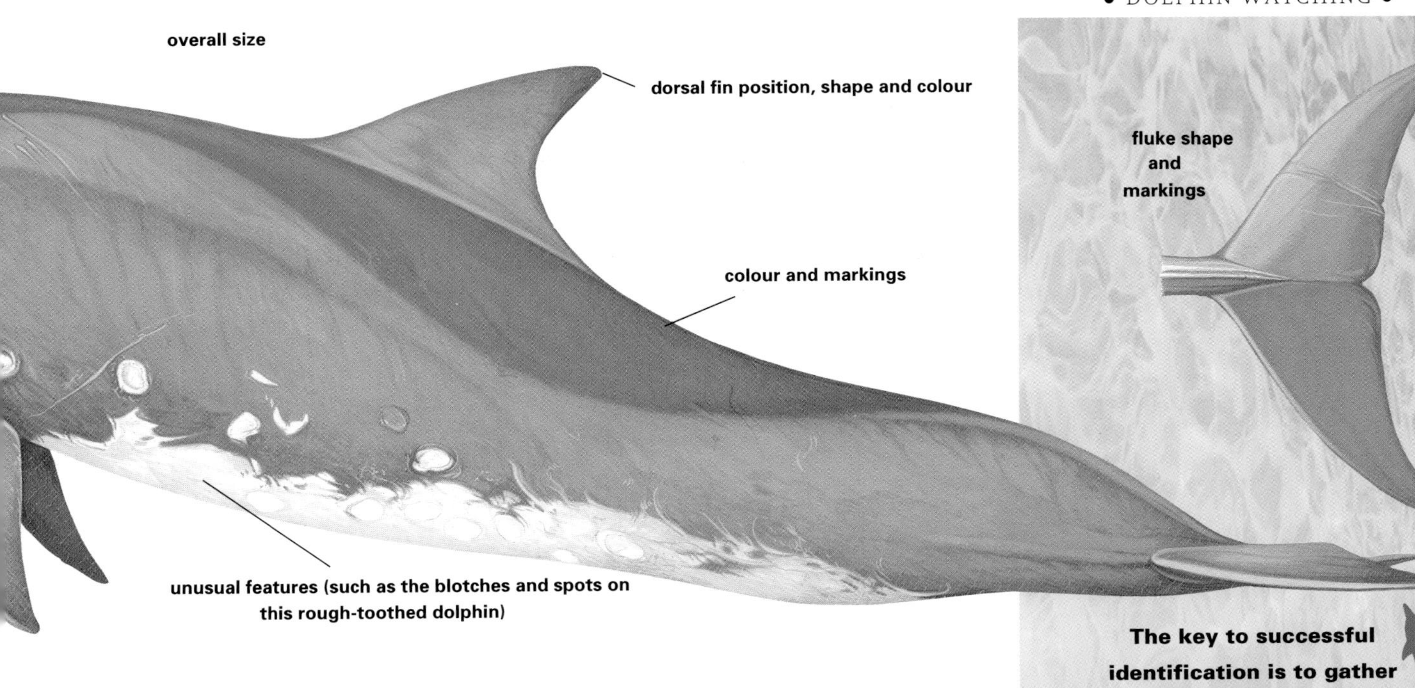

The key to successful identification is to gather information on as many different features and characteristics as possible before drawing any conclusions. In addition to the physical features shown here, bear in mind the surfacing and dive sequence, breaching or any other interesting behaviour, the number of animals together, and the location.

No two dolphins are exactly alike – even if they belong to the same species. Apart from scarring, and other distinctive markings gained over the years, their natural colouration often differs from one individual to the next. These two black dolphins, for example, belong to the same species but the extent of white on their 'lips' varies considerably.

CHAPTER

9

Save the Dolphin

Hundreds of thousands of dolphins around the world die every year as a direct result of human greed, laziness and ignorance. This is considerably more than all the great whales that were being killed at the height of the massacre that brought several species to the brink of extinction. Quite rightly, there has been a public outcry about the whales, and they have received a great deal of attention. Yet, until recently, the desperate plight of the world's dolphins has gone relatively unnoticed.

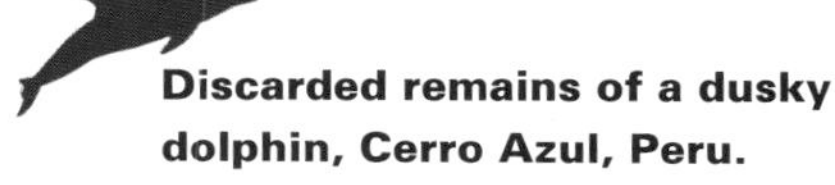

Discarded remains of a dusky dolphin, Cerro Azul, Peru.

Dolphin Hunting

Dolphins are hunted in many countries around the world, with nets, knives, rifles and hand-held harpoons. They are deliberately slaughtered for human consumption or to be used as crab bait, and they are ground into fertiliser and chicken food. Fishermen kill them in the belief that they damage their nets, and because they claim that dolphins are stealing or scaring away their fish (ironically, the scarcity of fish in many areas is caused by over-exploitation by the fishermen themselves; governments often turn a blind eye to the dolphin killing, rather than admit to the failure of their fishery policies).

The largest dolphin hunt on record used to take place in the Black Sea. During the decade between 1931–41, an astonishing 250,000–300,000 common dolphins and other small cetaceans were taken each year. The hunt was eventually stopped in 1966/67 by the Soviet Union, Romania and Bulgaria, but Turkey continued. In 1973, almost 130,000 animals were reportedly killed. Ten years later, in 1983, after a great deal of public pressure, the Turks officially ceased hunting, but the killing still continues illegally.

Some of the most barbaric hunts are the so-called 'drive-fisheries'. These are particularly common in Japan and, to a lesser extent, on some Pacific islands. Large schools of dolphins are driven into bays, while their escape routes are blocked by nets. The fishermen then wade from the beach into the shallow water and brutally massacre all the animals with long knives. In Japan, the meat from coastal hunts was traditionally sold for local consumption, but more now finds its way into city supermarkets and restaurants; the hunters are cashing in on the shortage and expense of whale meat by providing dolphin meat as a more affordable alternative.

The list of other countries with dolphin hunts (both legal and illegal) is almost endless, but includes South Africa, the Caribbean islands of St Vincent and St Lucia, the Azores, Papua New Guinea and Sri Lanka. In Sri Lanka alone, the inshore gillnet fisheries kill up to 42,000 spinner dolphins and other species every year; some of the deaths are accidental, but with recent declines in fish stocks, the number of dolphins being taken deliberately is increasing.

South America is a particular problem area. Fishermen in Chile kill thousands of Commerson's dolphins, Peale's dolphins, black dolphins and other species every year to provide bait for the commercial crab fishery. It is

Dusky dolphins are the prime target of hunts in Peru, where as many as 20,000 dolphins and porpoises are killed deliberately or accidentally every year. Hunting the animals is illegal – but the law is rarely enforced.

cheaper and more efficient than using fish as bait, because dolphin meat can stay in the water for three times longer – up to three days – before it disintegrates. The fishermen call the dolphins tontitas, or 'silly ones', because they are so friendly and easy to kill. Crab fishing is a lucrative business, as the crabs are exported to Europe and North America.

In Peru, as many as 20,000 dusky dolphins, Burmeister's porpoises and other species are killed every year by fishermen in at least sixty ports up and down the coast. The scale of the hunting is now so high there are fears that the local dolphin populations may not survive. After intense pressure from both national and international conservation groups, the Peruvian government finally banned dolphin hunting in 1990. However, the ban is purely cosmetic; the hunt has simply gone underground and even local policemen turn a blind eye to what is happening. In many ports, the fishermen now butcher the dolphins in their boats, smuggle the meat ashore and load it straight into refrigerator trucks destined for the capital, Lima. As with the Chilean crab fishery, it is a lucrative trade, and not just the result of necessity or ignorance.

Dolphins are being killed in almost all the seas and oceans of the world. Many of the hunts are rarely observed and poorly recorded, so the true extent of the problem is unknown. But it is likely that tens of thousands of dolphins and other small cetaceans – possibly even 100,000 or more – are being taken every year. Clearly, much greater legal protection (and practical enforcement) is essential, but there is also a desperate need for better fisheries management to deter the fishermen from hunting dolphins simply because fish are in short supply. There are no easy solutions, but one thing is certain: action needs to be taken sooner rather than later, or many more dolphin populations will disappear.

Dolphin hunting is often cruel and wasteful but, in many parts of the world, it also threatens the survival of local dolphin populations.

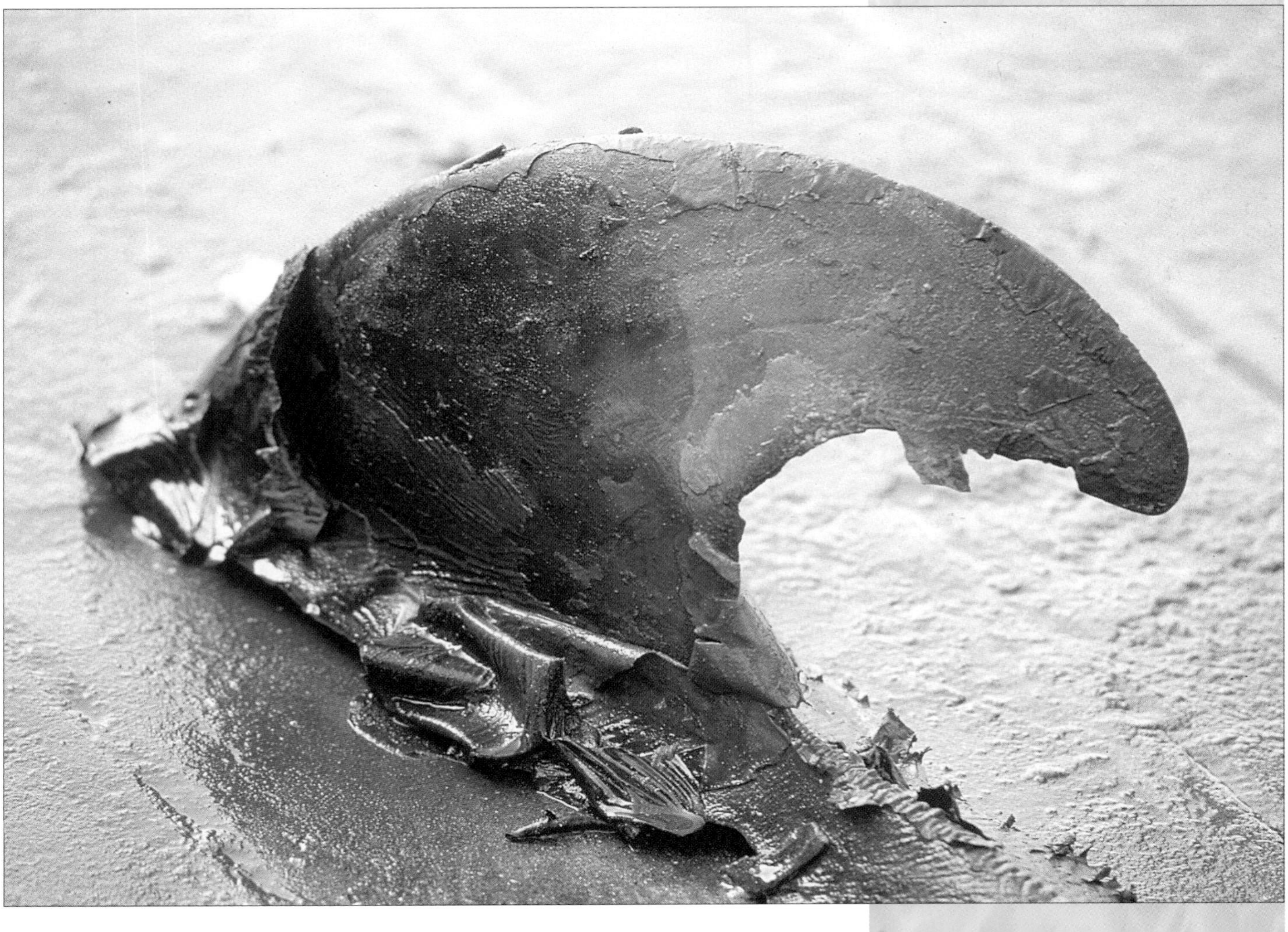

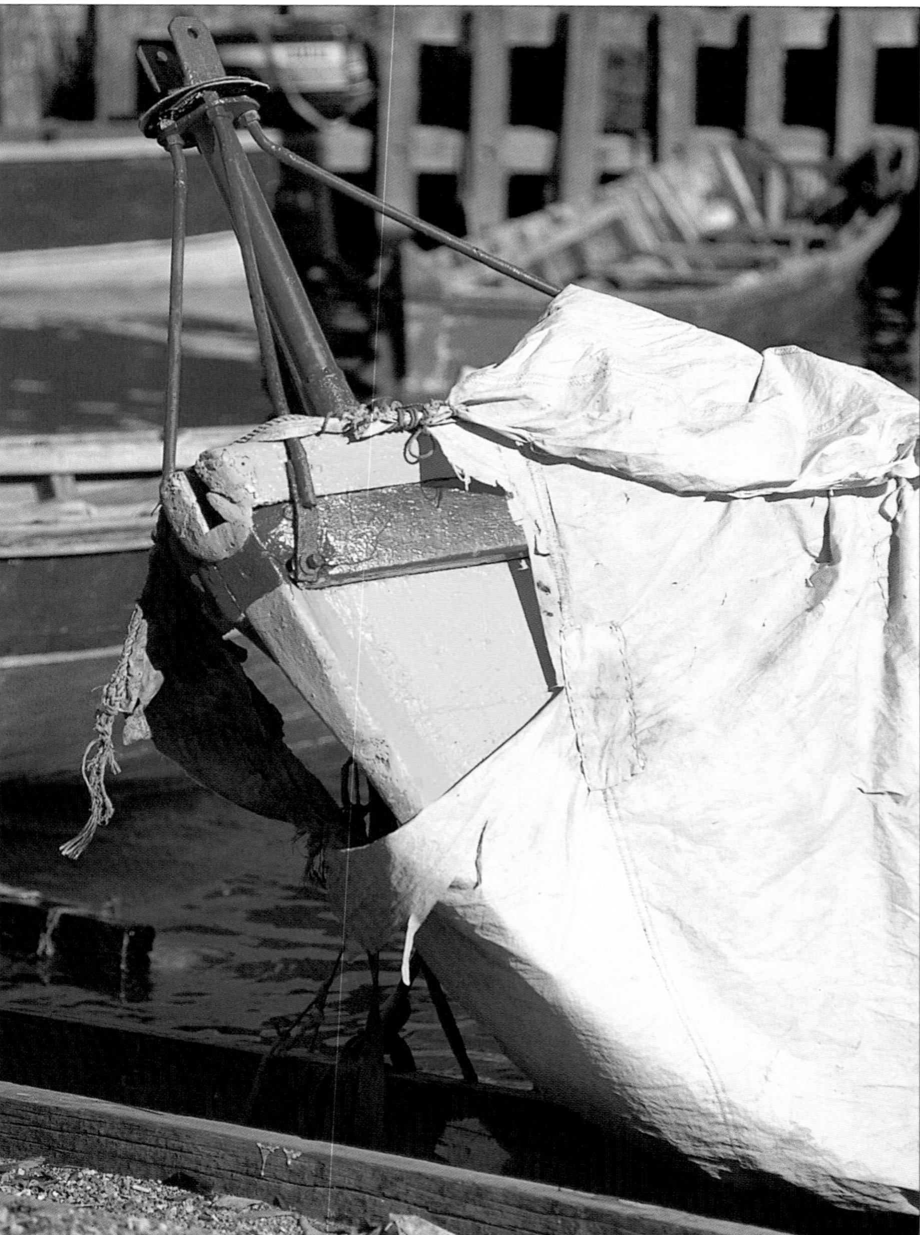

A variety of techniques are used to hunt dolphins around the world. On the Caribbean island of St Lucia, the bow of this wooden fishing boat has been fitted with a galvanised metal tripod; this is used to provide stability for a modified 12-gauge shotgun, which fires a harpoon.

Dolphin 'crisps' being prepared in the village of Barrouallie, on the Caribbean island of St Vincent. These are pieces of skin and blubber, deep fried in their own fat; they are normally eaten as a snack, as we would eat potato crisps.

Dolphins and Fisheries

Incredible though it may seem, the number of dolphins deliberately killed by hunters is almost minuscule compared to the number drowned in fishing nets around the world. Estimates of the magnitude of this carnage vary widely, but it is certainly counted in millions.

There are many commercial fishing techniques, but as far as oceanic dolphins are concerned three are particularly important: purse-seine netting, drift-netting and coastal gill-netting. Other techniques such as pelagic trawling and even long-lining are also dolphin killers, but the numbers involved are considerably smaller.

Tuna Fishing A particular form of purse-seine netting used by the tuna-fishing industry has killed more dolphins since it was introduced by the U.S. in 1959 than any other human activity. The slaughter has been both shocking and devastating, resulting in the deaths of an estimated six to twelve million dolphins over the past thirty-five years. Spotted and spinner dolphins have been the hardest hit – with some stocks declining by as much as 75 per cent – but common and Fraser's dolphins have also suffered frightening increases in mortality rate.

Staggering as they are, these figures are more than mere statistics. The suffering involved beggars belief. The dolphins die slow, lingering deaths in the nets after fruitlessly trying to break free and reach the surface to breathe. No-one knows how many of the animals that manage to escape, or are tossed back into the sea, later die from terrible injuries such as ruptured internal organs or torn flippers and flukes.

The main problem area is the eastern tropical Pacific (ETP), a stretch of ocean extending from southern California to Chile and covering an area roughly the size of Canada. As recently as the 1950s, tuna fishermen posed no threat to dolphins in the ETP, and still did their fishing near the coast with long lines and baited hooks. But with the introduction of giant purse-seine nets, the fishery was revolutionized. Small boats were quickly replaced with huge thrumming seiners that could travel anywhere in the open ocean, scoop up entire shoals of fish, and then carry catches of more than 1,200 tonnes back to shore.

Purse-seine fishermen soon began to use the presence of dolphins to find shoals of yellowfin tuna. They had known for some time that the two animals feed on the same small fish, and often swim together (although the precise reason is still unclear). Not only are dolphins much easier to find than tuna, because they have to keep surfacing for air, but the tuna associating with dolphins tend to be larger than average, and therefore command a higher market price. 'Fishing over porpoise', as the practice became known, began to increase tuna-fishing profits substantially.

The custom-built tuna boats became highly sophisticated and crammed with electronics. They began to carry their own helicopters to search for dolphins from the air. It became clear that no matter how violently the dolphins are herded and harassed, the fish continue to follow, and it is then simply a matter of slowing the animals down enough to catch them. A large net is pulled around the entire shoal and, once the animals are surrounded, the bottom is closed underneath to form a bag (like drawing shut the neck of an old-fashioned purse – hence the name purse-seine). As the drawstring is pulled tight and the net dragged towards the side of the seiner, the trapped dolphins panic. They rush at the net walls, getting tangled by their beaks, flippers and flukes, or are simply trapped underwater in great canopies of loose netting – and drown.

In the worst period, during the 1960s and early 1970s, it has been estimated that between 200,000 and 500,000 dolphins were being killed *every year* in the

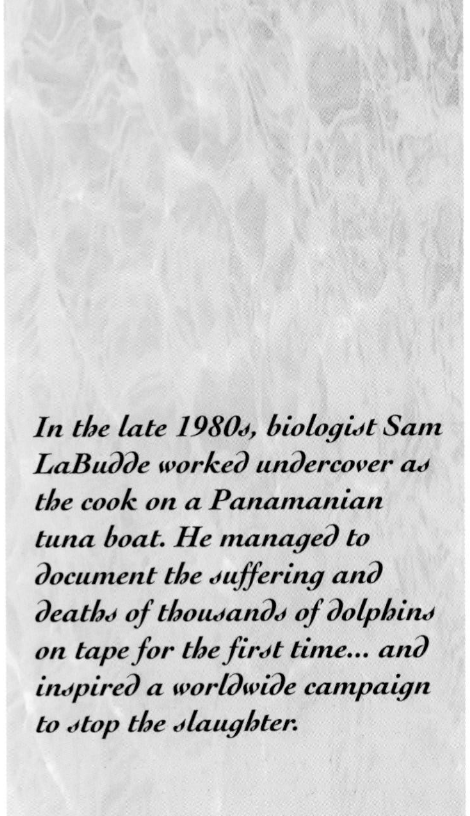

In the late 1980s, biologist Sam LaBudde worked undercover as the cook on a Panamanian tuna boat. He managed to document the suffering and deaths of thousands of dolphins on tape for the first time... and inspired a worldwide campaign to stop the slaughter.

ETP. The killing continues, although nowadays the scale of the problem is a great deal smaller. It has been suggested that the decline in mortality is partly because, after decades of slaughter, there are simply far fewer dolphins in the ETP than there were in the 1960s and 70s. This may be true, but the more likely explanation is that public outrage, and the determination of many conservation groups, has forced the introduction of crucial rules and regulations that now govern the tuna-fishing industry.

One of the most important early developments was the invention of a special panel of fine mesh, called the Medina panel after its inventor. Lying in a section of the net farthest from the vessel, this works as a kind of escape hatch that allows trapped dolphins to be released. It has significantly reduced the number of dolphin deaths, although bad weather and equipment malfunctions often

hamper the efforts of even the best-intentioned and most experienced crews. On one well-documented occasion, for example, the Medina panel could not be used properly and 736 dolphins drowned in a single 'set'.

However, the use of the Medina panel had to be enforced if it were to be effective, and the U.S. eventually bowed to tremendous public pressure with the introduction of the Marine Mammal Protection Act (MMPA) in 1972. The MMPA was responsible for several major improvements, and succeeded in achieving a small reduction in the number of dolphins being killed. In particular, it made use of the Medina panel compulsory for all U.S.-registered vessels and ruled that official observers had to be on board to count kills and report any infractions. However, while the original intention of the MMPA was to reduce the 'allowable' dolphin kill by U.S.-registered vessels over a period of years, this never really happened. Ronald Reagan submitted to the powerful economic and political lobby of the tuna industry, and relaxed the regulations; meanwhile, more than half the U.S.-registered tuna boats reacted badly to the MMPA – and subsequent rulings – by 'going foreign'. In order to free

Fishermen frequently blame dolphins for declining fish stocks but, ironically, it is over-exploitation by the fishermen themselves that is usually to blame.

In Sri Lanka alone, it is estimated that at least 40,000 dolphins die in coastal gill-nets every year.

themselves from the regulations, they began to appear under the flags of other countries such as Panama, Costa Rica, Mexico and Venezuela. So the problem was simply passed along, as the officially regulated U.S. fleet shrank in size and the unregulated foreign fleet grew.

With large numbers of dolphins still being killed, the U.S. urged the body responsible for managing the ETP tuna-fishing industry to take action of its own. Known as the Inter-American Tropical Tuna Commission (IATTC), this body was originally set up by the U.S. and Costa Rica, in 1949, to conserve tuna. Its members now include most (but not all) of the countries engaged in purse-seine tuna-fishing in the ETP.

The IATTC was in an ideal position to tackle the tuna–dolphin issue and, in 1976, broadened its responsibilities to take the issue into account. Ten years later, in 1986, it introduced an official observer programme that allows experts to be placed on all vessels capable of fishing for tuna in association with dolphins in the ETP. The experts' role is to gather detailed information for several purposes: for statistics and basic research on dolphins, for the enforcement of national regulations and for a basis of the 'dolphin-safe' or 'dolphin-friendly' label now used by some tuna processors. They are also encouraged to develop techniques for catching tuna that do not harm dolphins, and to provide training for crews of the international tuna-fishing fleet.

A major development came in 1992, when IATTC member governments signed an agreement designed to reduce dolphin mortality in the ETP to levels approaching zero. Known as the 1992 Agreement for the Conservation of Dolphins, or simply the La Jolla Agreement, its main objective was to reduce the annual mortality of dolphins without harming the tuna resources of the region or the fisheries which depend on them. Since it came into effect, in January 1993, it has decreased the permissible dolphin mortality each year; the overall limit has been apportioned among vessels participating in the fishery, and any vessel reaching its limit has had to stop fishing 'on dolphins' for the rest of the year.

'Our best hope for conserving cetaceans may be our almost natural love for them.'

BERND WÜRSIG
MARINE BIOLOGIST

The La Jolla Agreement included a target reduction in dolphin mortality in the ETP from 19,500 in 1993 to less than 5,000 by 1999. It has been an enormous success: the death toll in 1994 was estimated to be 4,095. This is still too high, of course, and conservation groups are continuing to lobby for a reduction in dolphin deaths to zero, but it is nevertheless a dramatic improvement. Unfortunately, there is now mounting evidence to suggest that dolphins are being set on by tuna-fishing fleets in other parts of the world, outside the ETP – so the problem could be repeating itself.

The real irony is that there are ways of catching tuna without putting the dolphins at such high risk. One, called long-lining, involves hanging thousands of baited hooks from lines (often several kilometres long) to attract the fish. Another is log-fishing, which takes advantage of the fact that tuna frequently gather under floating objects such as logs; the shoals involved can be remarkably large, and they are already being 'set upon' by some purse-seiners.

'Dolphin-safe' Tuna Meanwhile, the world's largest tuna company, under pressure from an international consumer boycott, launched the first 'dolphin-safe' or 'dolphin-friendly' tuna in 1990. Many other tuna companies around the world quickly followed suit. Unfortunately, despite the efforts of the IATTC observers, there is still no independent enforcement scheme for checking such claims, and already some of the less-reputable tuna companies have been caught cheating. Yet most of the world's tuna comes from outside the ETP, and is caught using relatively safe fishing techniques – so there is absolutely no excuse for continuing such appalling and unnecessary animal slaughter.

The dolphins killed during tuna-fishing operations are frequently described as

an 'incidental catch'. This is an extremely misleading term, concealing the fact that they are *intentionally* located, chased and encircled with fishing nets. However, most other fishing techniques really do catch dolphins incidentally. The numbers caught are still staggeringly high – probably amounting to hundreds of thousands every year – but the difference is that the dolphins are not being targeted on purpose. Incidental catches have been happening since at least the Middle Ages, but they have only become a major problem in the last thirty or forty years. The introduction of increasingly destructive fishing methods – designed to achieve maximum short-term profits – is mainly to blame.

Chilean fishermen call dolphins and porpoises 'tontitas', or 'silly ones', because they are so friendly and easy to kill. They harpoon and shoot the animals illegally to use their meat for crab fishing (fish is the official crab bait, but dolphin meat is much cheaper and lasts for longer in the water).

Drift-netting Drift-netting was first used widely in the mid-1960s and has rapidly become another major worldwide threat to dolphins. It is basically a way of stripmining the oceans, and is probably the most indiscriminate method of fishing ever devised. Drift nets are strung out in long lines, each with a series of corks along the top and weights along the bottom, and hang in the water like invisible curtains. They can be placed at different depths, but are normally used to catch shoaling fish such as herring or anchovy in the top 15 metres (50 feet) of the water column. Normally released at dusk, they are allowed to drift with the ocean's currents and winds before being retrieved the following day.

It is hard to imagine, but a single drift net can measure up to 50 kilometres (30 miles) long. There are literally thousands upon thousands of kilometres of drift nets floating around the world's seas and oceans at any one time – more than enough to circle the earth at the equator. They catch everything in their path, from sharks and other non-target fish to seabirds and turtles. Literally anything that moves near the nets is likely to be caught and killed. They are made of such fine strands of nylon that even dolphins cannot detect them with their remarkably sensitive sonar, and consequently are killed in frightening numbers. Not surprisingly, drift nets have been dubbed 'walls of death' or 'curtains of death'.

There has been some success in regulating the use of drift nets, albeit fairly limited, and some countries at least are recognizing their extreme danger. In January 1992, for example, the European Commission (EC) banned all member nations from using nets over 2.5 kilometres (1½ miles) long. This was a major

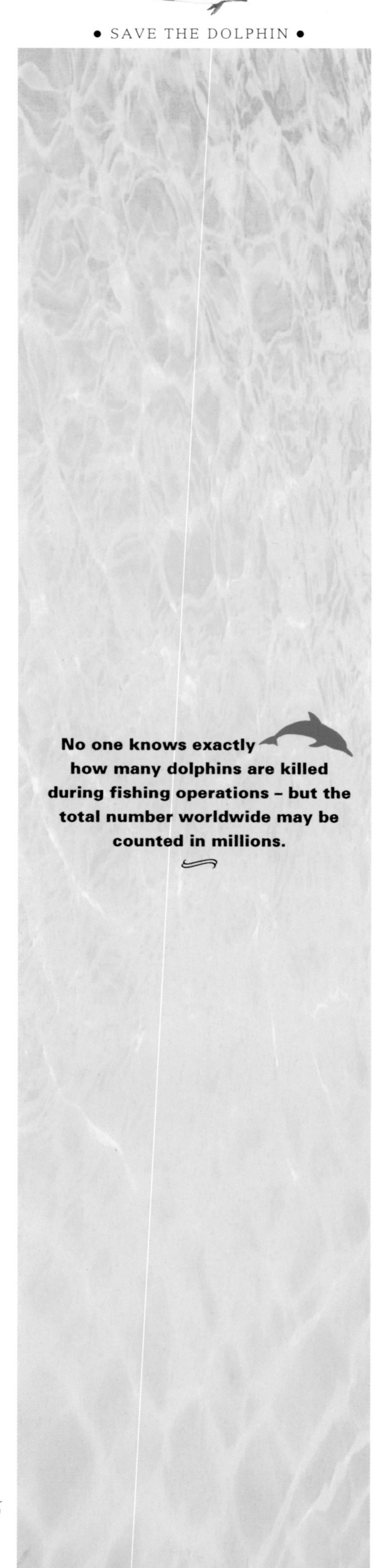

No one knows exactly how many dolphins are killed during fishing operations – but the total number worldwide may be counted in millions.

step in the right direction, although France was granted an extension until June 1994 to phase out its longer nets. Then the French applied for yet another extension and the European Union (EU) began to hedge its bets. Other countries took advantage of the wrangling and promptly began to use their long nets again. Thousands of dolphins died unnecessarily as a direct result of the EU's bureaucratic feebleness. But eventually, in the summer of 1994, under pressure from conservation groups, the French were forced to come into line, and have since agreed to abide by the EU ban.

Coastal Gill-netting and Trawling Many coastal fishermen use nets which are similar to drift nets in design. They are much shorter, and have to be anchored on the bottom in relatively shallow water, but are made with the same thin nylon monofilament line. This is knotted to form a meshed net which, as in ocean-going drift nets, is nearly invisible underwater. When a fish attempts to swim through the mesh it becomes entangled, usually by the gills – hence the name 'coastal gill-net'.

Cheap and durable coastal gill-nets were originally developed to provide an affordable and effective fishing method for developing countries, and work very well. However, it is almost impossible for dolphins to detect them using sonar, and a great many drown in these death-traps every year. They may even be attracted to the nets by the abundance of trapped fish and, unaware of the weak echo from the thin mesh until it is too late, become entangled themselves. Species inhabiting coastal waters, especially in heavily fished areas, are most at risk. There is no way of knowing the total numbers killed

because there are no figures for most countries, but it is a worldwide problem stretching from New Zealand to Sri Lanka and from Canada to the UK.

In comparison, trawling with funnel-shaped nets pulled along by one or two boats is less of a problem for dolphins. Originally, trawling was designed to catch species that live in deep water or inhabit the ocean floor, such as cod and flatfish. This is known as 'bottom trawling' and, while it can have detrimental effects on the seabed, it catches relatively few dolphins. A fast-growing concern is 'pelagic trawling' in mid-water, although little is known about its potential dangers for non-target species.

Over-exploitation of Fish Stocks The indirect impact that fisheries may have on dolphin populations through over-exploitation of fish stocks is also important, but this is extremely difficult to measure because there are many variables involved. However, there is more than enough circumstantial evidence to ring alarm bells. Decades of over-exploitation of herring, mackerel, sprat and other fish stocks in the North Sea, for example, may be at least partly responsible for the comparative scarcity of dolphins and other cetaceans in the region.

We are still far from identifying all the problems caused by fishing operations, let alone measuring their precise impact or enforcing practical solutions. In some cases, a simple modification of either the nets or the fishery management system can have a positive effect. Scaring the dolphins away with acoustic 'scarecrows', or making the nets more detectable, may work in some cases, but much more drastic action is needed if we are to counteract the immense threats posed by the sheer scale of many modern commercial fisheries.

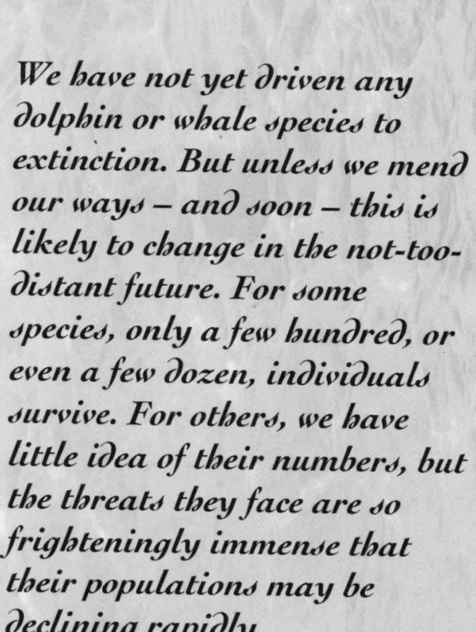

We have not yet driven any dolphin or whale species to extinction. But unless we mend our ways – and soon – this is likely to change in the not-too-distant future. For some species, only a few hundred, or even a few dozen, individuals survive. For others, we have little idea of their numbers, but the threats they face are so frighteningly immense that their populations may be declining rapidly.

Pollution

Pollution tends to be a less-emotive subject than hunting or drowning in fishing nets, but it is nevertheless a silent, and often invisible, killer that seriously threatens dolphin populations around the world. Despite all the warnings, we continue to dump mind-boggling quantities of untreated sewage, industrial waste, agricultural chemicals, modern plastic debris and a huge variety of other pollutants into the sea. We are only just beginning to learn about the details of the damage being caused, but already some experts predict that pollution could be the most serious threat to the future survival of dolphins and other cetaceans.

Many governments choose to ignore the severity of the situation. They think only in the short-term, with a 'dump-it-now, worry-about-the-effects-later' approach. The fact that many pollutants – even if they were banned today – would remain in the marine environment and still be dangerous for many years to come makes such a cavalier attitude all the more frightening.

The world's oceans are being used as dustbins for toxic chemicals, heavy metals, untreated sewage and all our other waste products.

Dolphins are particularly vulnerable to pollution, not least because of their position near the top of the food chain. This means that they build up higher concentrations of pollutants in their bodies than many other animals; minute quantities of toxins in the sea are picked up by marine plankton, which are then ingested by fish and squid, which in turn are ingested by dolphins and other top predators. As they get older, more and more pollutants accumulate in their blubber and other fat reserves in their bodies. This build-up is even

passed on from one generation of dolphins to another – a lactating female can deliver the toxins in highly concentrated doses to her calf through her milk.

Dolphins living along the coast are particularly vulnerable, because they come into close contact with exceptionally large quantities and a wide range of pollutants. The species and populations in semi-enclosed waters, such as the Baltic Sea, Mediterranean Sea, North Sea, Gulf of Mexico and Gulf of St Lawrence, are particularly hard-hit. Indeed, in some areas, contaminant levels in cetaceans are so high that their bodies could be classified as toxic waste.

Oil The seas have been used as a dumping ground for a variety of pollutants for many years. Oil was one of the first to come to public attention. Large spills such as the Torrey Canyon, Amoco Cadiz, Exxon Valdez, Bahia Paraiso and Braer have made headline news around the world. Acute accidents such as these can be particularly catastrophic – after the Exxon Valdez disaster in Prince William Sound, Alaska, in 1989, for example, oil covered an estimated area of 15,445 square kilometres (9,600 square miles). However, most oil – sometimes millions of tons every year – enters the sea through the cleaning of the ships' bilge tanks and other routine uncontrolled discharges. This may be less dramatic than major oil spills and rarely, if ever, makes the headlines, but it is no less harmful.

Hundreds of thousands of plastic items are dumped into the world's oceans every day. They pose a serious threat to dolphins, which may swallow plastic bags or get tangled up in other garbage – and die slowly of strangulation or starvation.

Limited evidence suggests that dolphins may avoid thick oil spills, by swimming round them, but they have been observed travelling straight through light sheens of oil on the surface. Even this exposes them to highly volatile toxic fumes, which may cause inflammation of their mucous membranes, lung congestion and pneumonia, and ultimately could induce liver damage and neurological disorders.

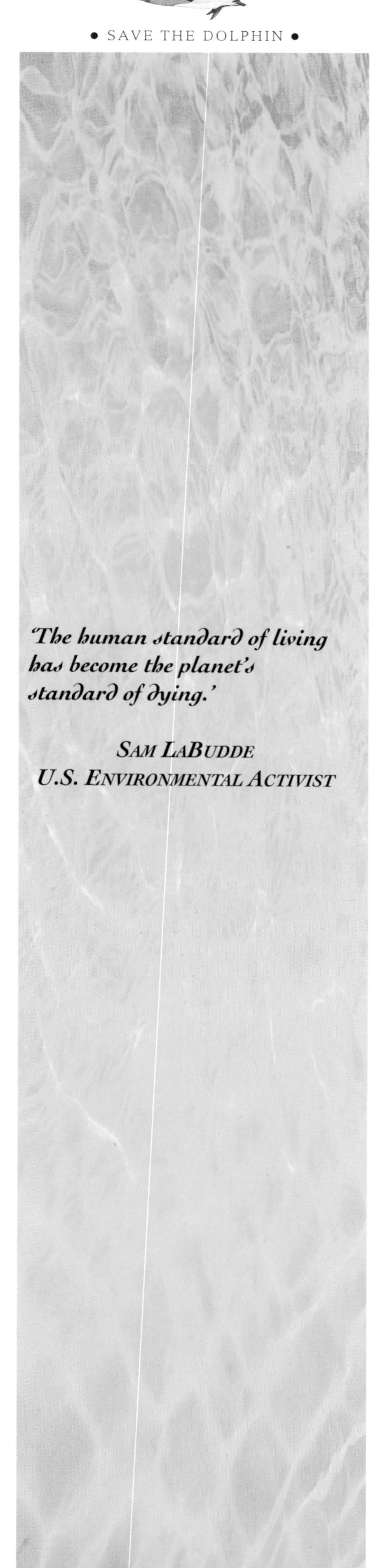

'The human standard of living has become the planet's standard of dying.'

Sam LaBudde
U.S. Environmental Activist

Chemical Waste Nowadays, there is particular concern about agricultural and industrial organochlorines and heavy metals. These include organochlorine pesticides such as DDT, mirex, endrin, and dieldrin (generally referred to as chlorinated hydrocarbons), industrial organochlorines such as polychlorinated biphenyls (PCBs), and heavy metals such as mercury, lead, cadmium and zinc. Many of these deadly toxins are discharged or dumped directly into the sea, while others find their way via agricultural run-offs and atmospheric deposition. Once they have entered the sea, of course, it is too late – they can neverbe recovered.

Organochlorines have been used widely in agriculture and industry since the 1920s. Their toxicity was first recognized some forty years later (ironically when production reached a peak), by which time a great deal of damage had already been done. Tight controls have been introduced in Western Europe and North America, but they are still manufactured and discharged in other parts of world – and they are so persistent that they will remain in the environment for a long time to come. Since organochlorines are hardly soluble in water, but dissolve readily in fat, they are stored in the fatty tissues of animals' bodies. This is why small amounts eaten regularly can quickly build up to dangerously high levels.

PCBs have been used commercially since the 1930s, in a wide range of products from electric transformers to adhesives. Their toxic effects were first documented as early as 1936, but it was not until the late 1960s that the dangers of using them were fully and widely appreciated. They are no longer being produced, but it has been estimated that 1.5 million tonnes of PCBs had already been made by the time production stopped. A third has already leaked into the environment – mostly into the sea, where it has reached even the remotest corners of the world. The remainder is still in use, is being held in cold storage or has been dumped in landfills (PCBs are immensely stable, and can be destroyed only through incineration at extremely high temperatures). There is serious concern that if many more PCBs find their way into the sea, they could cause mass extinctions of marine mammals and other wildlife.

There have been a number of warnings about the potential dangers of PCBs. In 1990, for example, thousands (or, possibly, even tens of thousands) of striped dolphins died in the Mediterranean as a result of a distemper virus. They were found to have exceptionally high levels of PCBs in their bodies. Whether this was pure coincidence, or whether it was the indirect cause of death, we will probably never know. Large numbers of dolphins have died, many in mysterious circumstances as the victims of unexplained viruses or weakened immune systems, in several parts of the world in recent years. The possibilities are ominous.

Heavy metals have a wide range of chemical properties and biological effects, yet millions of tonnes of them are dumped into the environment every year. Human activities such as mining, smelting, waste dumping, rubbish burning and the addition of lead to petrol are to blame. Many heavy metals have no biological function, and their presence in all but very small quantities can cause poisoning. Like organochlorines, they tend to build up in the tissues of living organisms – often with devastating effect. In the 1950s, for example, hundreds of Japanese people died or were permanently crippled after eating mercury-contaminated fish; the mercury had been discharged from a local chemical plant.

Sewage Raw untreated human sewage, with its cocktail of potentially harmful diseases, is discharged into the sea from towns and villages all over the world. Coastal communities are all too often tempted to pump their domestic wastes into a seemingly all-absorbing sea, as it simply outweighs the cost of adequate sewage treatment plants.

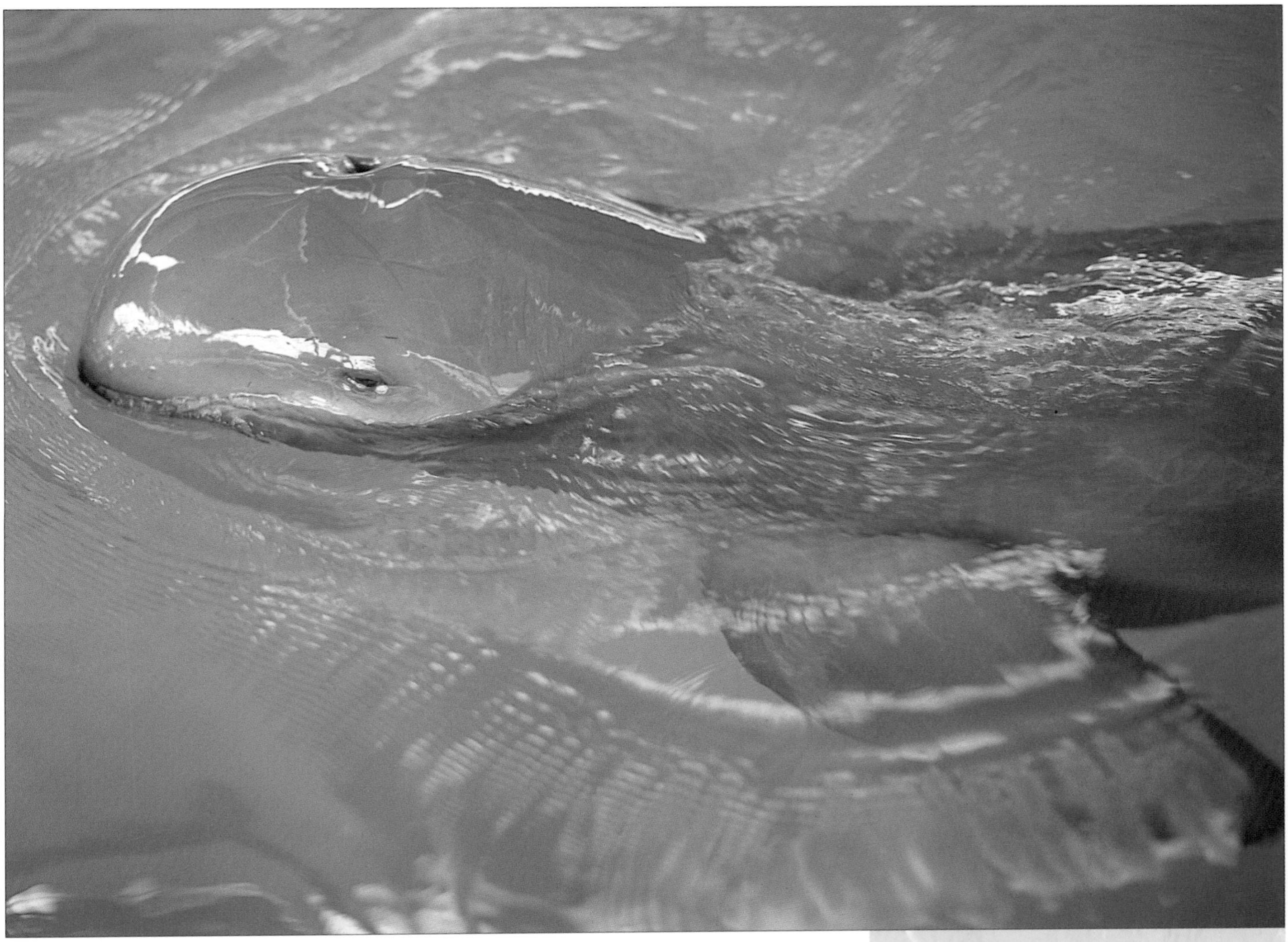

Pollution, especially from logging operations, is destroying the habitat and food resources of the Irrawaddy dolphin in many parts of south-east Asia.

Rubbish The damaging effect of rubbish is perhaps more obvious than it is for many of the more 'invisible' pollutants. Lost or deliberately discarded fishing gear poses the biggest threat; the dolphins get tangled up, and drown, or strangle themselves in their struggle to break free. A piece of fishing line caught around a dolphin's neck will slowly cut deeper into its flesh, and can take days, weeks or even months to kill. But apparently innocent items like plastic bags, bottles and even the rings holding six-packs together can also be killers, and are especially dangerous because of their durability, transparency and the fact that they float. Plastic bags, for example, are sometimes swallowed in mistake for squid. It has been estimated that as many as half a million items of plastic are dumped into the world's oceans every day.

It is difficult to measure exactly how much damage all these pollutants are doing to dolphin populations. The quantities involved are often unknown, their effects depend upon everything from the type of pollutant to the length of exposure, and most of the victims die at sea. Measurements are also complicated by the fact that, while the initial damage is frighteningly varied and insidious, it may not cause immediate death. Instead, it gradually weakens the dolphins with hormonal imbalances, loss of fertility, a lowering of disease resistance, brain damage and various neurological disorders, cancer, liver troubles, and a wide range of other abnormalities and chronic health problems. Despite all the unknowns, few experts dispute that the overall damage is likely to be substantial. In fact, it is precisely because of all the unknowns that we should be especially cautious – and make determined efforts to do something about the potential problems.

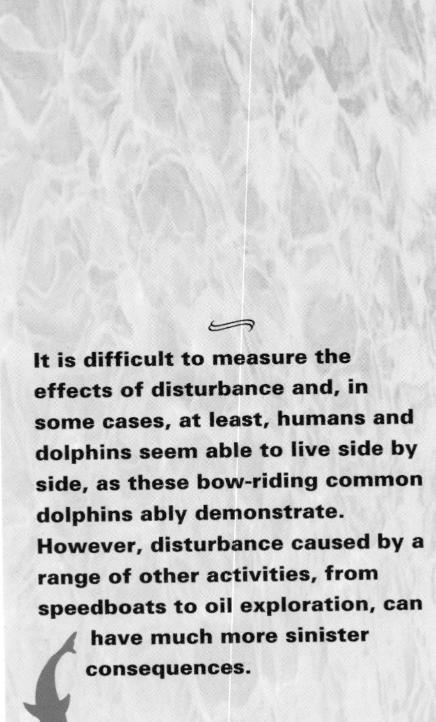

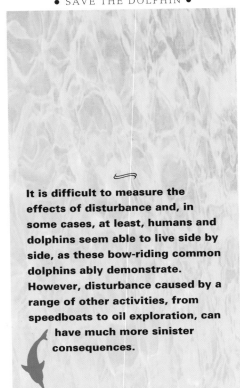

It is difficult to measure the effects of disturbance and, in some cases, at least, humans and dolphins seem able to live side by side, as these bow-riding common dolphins ably demonstrate. However, disturbance caused by a range of other activities, from speedboats to oil exploration, can have much more sinister consequences.

Habitat Degradation and Disturbance

Dolphins living close to shore or near human activities at sea often have to contend with a variety of additional problems. These include coastal development, disturbance from boat traffic, and noise pollution. Unfortunately, many of the species most affected have restricted distributions and are tied to coastal areas, so they cannot easily escape.

Habitat degradation and destruction have probably caused more extinctions on land than any other human pressure. The situation at sea is rather different, and more limited, but as the natural coastline in many parts of the world is replaced with an ever-growing number of marinas, harbours, hotel complexes and other developments, it is becoming increasingly important.

One of the many problems associated with coastal development is an increase in boat traffic. Many coastal areas, as well as major shipping lanes, have seen a dramatic increase in the number of vessels in recent years. Some of the effects are obvious – boats and ships collide with dolphins or injure them with their propellers. But there is also a general level of disturbance that can be even more damaging. The main concern is not so much dolphins having to take evasive action once in a while, or brief spells of aberrant behaviour, but the forcible exclusion of entire populations from important feeding and breeding grounds or migration routes.

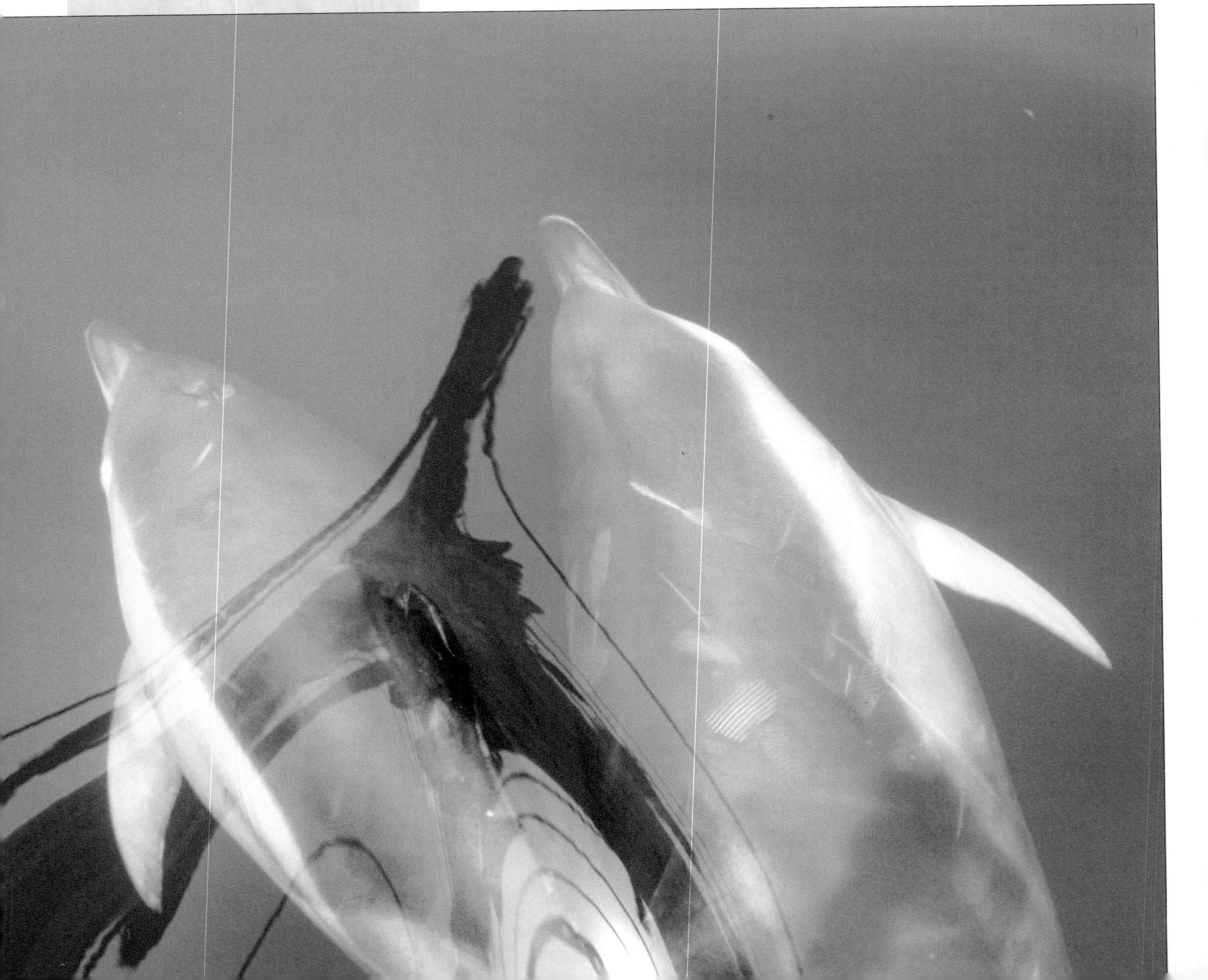

Increased boat traffic brings with it an increase in noise. Since dolphins rely so heavily on sound to interpret their environment, and to communicate with one another, they are believed to be especially vulnerable to this form of disturbance. It is not only the loudness of a noise that is important. Its frequency has to be taken into consideration as well, since some frequencies are likely to be more of a problem for dolphins than others. Their greatest hearing sensitivity is 1–150 kHz (although they can hear down to about 20 Hz) and so pleasure craft and other vessels which generate sounds within this range are particularly troublesome. A great deal depends upon sea conditions, bottom topography, water depth, the position of the dolphin in the water column and a variety of other factors, but as sound travels so well underwater many boats can be heard from a distance of several kilometres.

Industrial activities such as oil and gas exploration are another source of extraneous noise and general disturbance. Seismic testing, drilling and production sounds, and the noise of aircraft and vessels visiting installations are all likely to affect dolphins in one way or another.

Ironically, there is growing concern that in some areas dolphin watching is becoming another source of disturbance. Again, it is inshore dolphins that are suffering the most, simply because they are more readily accessible. There is no doubt that too many boats chasing after too few dolphins can be a major problem, and in parts of the world where there is a dolphin-watching free-for-all with no regulations, it is already a problem that needs to be tackled as a matter of urgency (see Chapter 8).

It is easy to imagine that dolphins escape the ravages of habitat destruction that threaten so many terrestrial animals – yet many species are suffering as the world's natural coastlines are replaced by marinas, harbours, seaside resorts and other major developments.

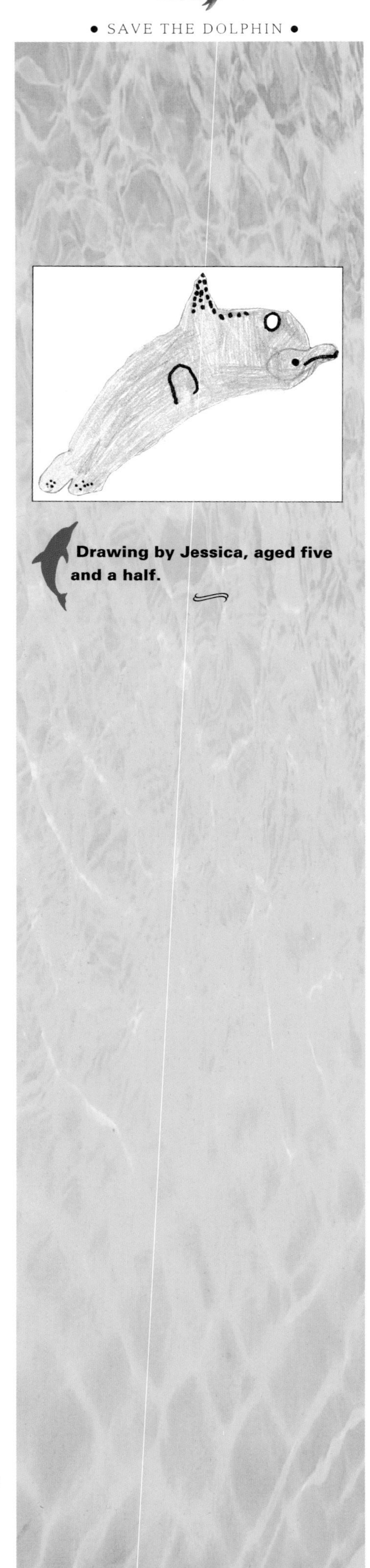

Drawing by Jessica, aged five and a half.

The Future

Dolphins face so many threats that it is not surprising to find all the species described in this book listed in *The IUCN Red List of Threatened Animals*, compiled by the World Conservation Monitoring Centre. No dolphin has become extinct in modern times – as far as we are aware – but a number are considered to be at risk, and others have all but disappeared from many of their former haunts. The odds are firmly stacked against them and, considering the magnitude of the problems they face, for some the future is bleak.

However, there is hope. There have been some major conservation successes in recent years – the tuna-fishing issue immediately comes to mind – and there has been enormous growth in our awareness and knowledge of the conservation needs of many dolphin species.

There has also been a surge of public interest. One of the most encouraging signs is the growing number of children taking an active interest in dolphins and their conservation. In a recent newspaper survey among British children, dolphins were voted the most popular animals – beating much-loved giant

pandas and dinosaurs to the number one position. In fact, these days, many youngsters know so much about dolphins, and are so aware of other wildlife and conservation issues, that they are teaching their parents.

The most effective way for an individual to help is by lending support to organizations that are fighting to save dolphins around the world, such as the Whale and Dolphin Conservation Society. With sufficient funding and public support, they can carry out the research essential to identify key problem areas, run field conservation projects, lobby governments, put pressure on companies that continue to exploit dolphins and carry out a variety of other crucial activities. A list of some of the organizations to join is provided in Appendix 2.

We recognize that there is something special about dolphins; we see them as we would like to see ourselves. And we realize that we are causing them harm; so much harm, in fact, that their very existence is under threat. Yet we still have not learned from the mistakes of the past. If we cannot live in harmony with such intelligent, charismatic and peaceable creatures as dolphins, we will probably find that we are unable to live in harmony with nature at all.

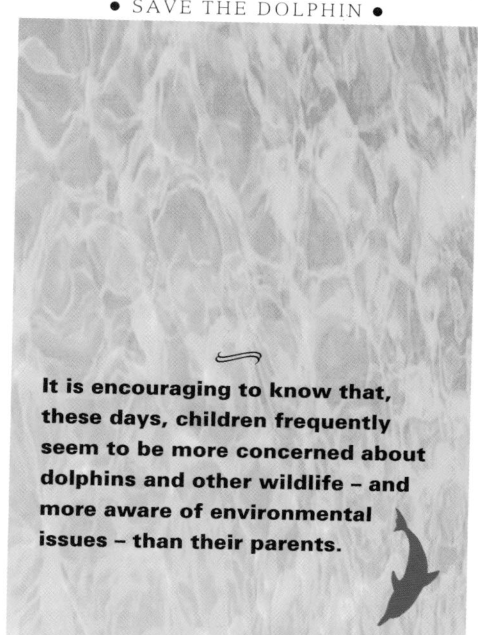

It is encouraging to know that, these days, children frequently seem to be more concerned about dolphins and other wildlife – and more aware of environmental issues – than their parents.

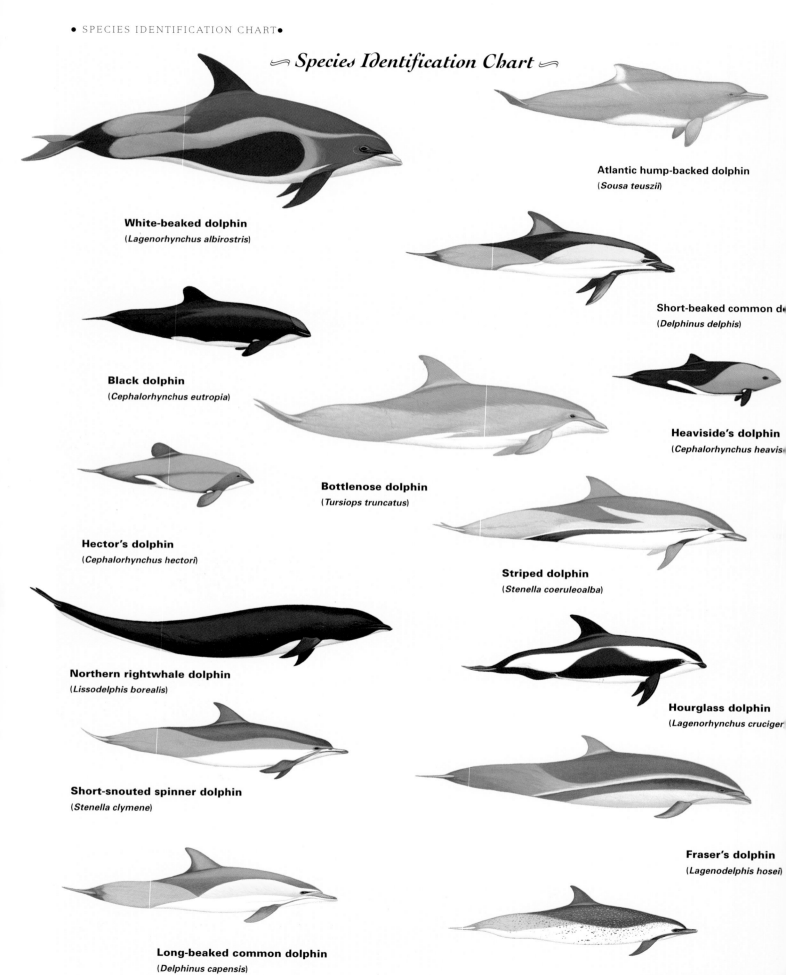

Species Identification Chart

White-beaked dolphin
(*Lagenorhynchus albirostris*)

Black dolphin
(*Cephalorhynchus eutropia*)

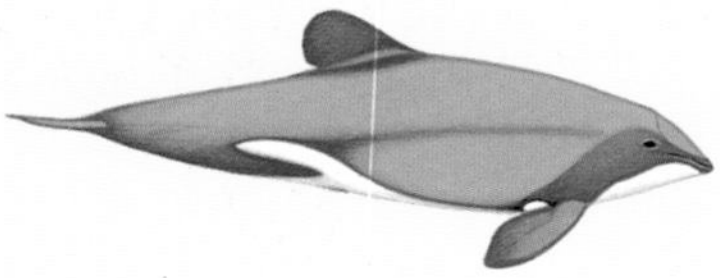

Hector's dolphin
(*Cephalorhynchus hectori*)

Bottlenose dolphin
(*Tursiops truncatus*)

Northern rightwhale dolphin
(*Lissodelphis borealis*)

Short-snouted spinner dolphin
(*Stenella clymene*)

Long-beaked common dolphin
(*Delphinus capensis*)

Atlantic hump-backed dolphin
(*Sousa teuszii*)

Short-beaked common d
(*Delphinus delphis*)

Heaviside's dolphin
(*Cephalorhynchus heavis*

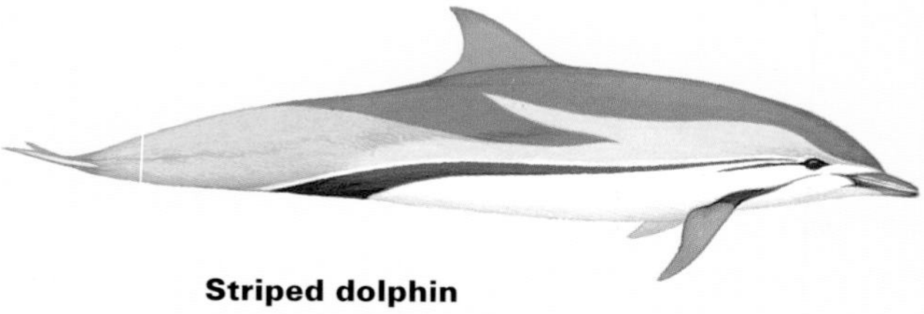

Striped dolphin
(*Stenella coeruleoalba*)

Hourglass dolphin
(*Lagenorhynchus cruciger*

Fraser's dolphin
(*Lagenodelphis hosei*)

Pantropical spotted dolp
(*Stenella attenuata*)

rrawaddy dolphin
(Orcaella brevirostris)

Dusky dolphin
(Lagenorhynchus obscurus)

Tucuxi
(Sotalia fluviatilis)

Indo-Pacific hump-backed dolphin
(Sousa chinensis)

Southern rightwhale dolphin
(Lissodelphis peronii)

Risso's dolphin
(Grampus griseus)

nmerson's dolphin
halorhynchus commersonii)

Rough-toothed dolphin
(Steno bredanensis)

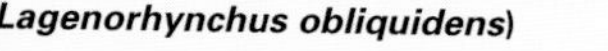

Pacific white-sided dolphin
(Lagenorhynchus obliquidens)

Atlantic white-sided dolphin
(Lagenorhynchus acutus)

Long-snouted spinner dolphin
(Stenella longirostris)

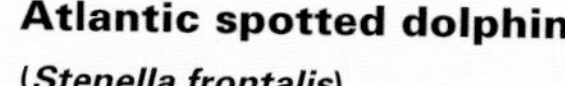

Atlantic spotted dolphin
(Stenella frontalis)

Peale's dolphin
(Lagenorhynchus australis)

Note: a further six species are included in the oceanic dolphin family, the Delphinidae. Known as the blackfish, they are unlike the other dolphins in appearance and, as in this book, are often treated separately. They are: the pygmy killer whale *(Feresa attenuata)*, the short-finned pilot whale *(Globicephala macrorhynchus)*, the long-finned pilot whale *(Globicephala melas)*, the killer whale *(Orcinus orca)*, the melon-headed whale *(Peponocephala electra)*, and the false killer whale *(Pseudorca crassidens)*.

How You Can Help

If you feel moved to help the world's dolphins, these are some of the organizations to support.

Whale and Dolphin Conservation Society (WDCS)
Alexander House, James Street West
Bath, Avon BA1 2BT, UK

International Dolphin Watch (IDW)
Parklands, North Ferriby
Humberside HU14 3ET, UK

Royal Society for the Prevention of Cruelty to Animals (RSPCA)
Causeway, Horsham
West Sussex RH12 1HG, UK

Marine Conservation Society (MCS)
9 Gloucester Road, Ross-on-Wye
Hereford and Worcester HR9 017, UK

World Wide Fund for Nature International (WWF)
CH-1196 Gland, Switzerland

Friends of the Dolphin
PO Box 337, Thornhill
Ontario, Canada L3T 4HZ

Australians for Animals
PO Box 673, Byron Bay
New South Wales 2481, Australia

Project Interlock
PO Box 20, Whangarel
New Zealand

Dolphin Action and Protection Group
PO Box 2227, Fish Hoek 7975
South Africa

Greenpeace USA
1436 U Street, N.W.
Washington, DC 20009, USA

American Cetacean Society
PO Box 1391
San Pedro, CA 90733, USA

Cetacean Society International
21 Laurel Hill Road
Ridgefield, CT 06877, USA

Further Reading

Carwardine, Mark, *Eyewitness Handbooks: Whales, Dolphins and Porpoises*, Dorling Kindersley, London, 1995.
Catton, Chris, *Dolphins*, Boxtree, London, 1995.
Dobbs, Horace, *Dance to a Dolphin's Song*, Jonathan Cape, London, 1990.
Donoghue, Michael, and Wheeler, Annie, *Dolphins: Their Life and Survival*, Blandford, Auckland, 1990.
Evans, Peter, *Dolphins*, Whittet Books, London, 1994.
Harrison, R. and Ridgeway, Sam H., (eds), *Handbook of Marine Mammals Volume 5: The First Book of Dolphins*, Academic Press, London, 1994.
Hoyt, Erich, *Riding with the Dolphins – The Equinox Guide to Dolphins and Porpoises*, Camden House, Ontario, 1992.
Leatherwood, Stephen, and Reeves, Randall R., *The Sierra Club Handbook of Whales and Dolphins*, Sierra Club Books, San Francisco, 1983.
Martin, Anthony R., *Whales and Dolphins*, Salamander Books, London, 1990.
May, John, (ed), *The Greenpeace Book of Dolphins*, Century Editions, London, 1990.
Thompson, Paul, and Wilson, Ben, *Bottlenose Dolphins*, Colin Baxter Photography, Grantown-on-Spey, 1994.

Acknowledgements

The author would like to thank the many people who have helped with the research and production of this book. In particular, special thanks to the team at Dragon's World, especially Pippa Rubinstein, Jane Hurd-Cosgrave and John Strange, for their support, commitment to the project and professionalism; Alison Smith, Mark Simmonds and Chris Stroud at the Whale and Dolphin Conservation Society, for their invaluable comments on the original draft; and, of course, Martin Camm, for his friendship and enthusiasm – and, as always, for his exceptional artwork.

Index

Bold italic = illustrated text
Italic = illustration only